In My Kitchen

In My Kitchen

100 RECIPES FOR FOOD LOVERS, PASSIONATE COOKS, AND ENTHUSIASTIC EATERS

TED ALLEN

WITH BARRY RICE

CLARKSON POTTER/PUBLISHERS
NEW YORK

In memory of Dad. And pass the Cheez-Its.

Copyright © 2012 by Ted Allen
Photographs copyright © 2012 by Ben Fink

Published in the United States by Clarkson Potter/Publishers, an imprint of the
Crown Publishing Group, a division of Random House, Inc., New York.
www.crownpublishing.com
www.clarksonpotter.com

CLARKSON POTTER is a trademark and POTTER with colophon is a registered
trademark of Random House, Inc.

Library of Congress Cataloging-in-Publication Data
Allen, Ted.
   In My Kitchen / Ted Allen. — 1st ed.
   Includes index.
   1. Cooking, American.   2. Cookbooks.   I. Title.
   TX715.A442725 2012
   641.5973—dc23   2011029174

ISBN 978-0-307-95186-1

Printed in China

Design by Stephanie Huntwork

10 9 8 7 6 5 4 3 2 1

First Edition

Contents

Introduction

GOOGLE THE WORD *COOKBOOK* THESE DAYS, and you'll find all sorts of promises. There are recipes to shrink your waistline, save you money, improve your memory, increase your endurance—there's probably a cookbook out there that guarantees a full, lustrous head of hair. But more than anything else, most cookbooks seem to be about getting you out of the kitchen as quickly as possible: thirty-minute meals, five-minute meals, food that doesn't require cooking at all.

How about a cookbook for people who are *into* the kitchen? For people who, you know, *love* to cook?

Believe me, I understand the need for easy and speedy. After a twelve-hour day of shooting *Chopped,* say, I'm talking stir-fry, spaghetti, heck, peanut-butter sandwiches (more likely, I'm hitting the speed dial for pizza). But that's not about the joy of food. That's survival.

In this book, I'm talking about *this* kind of day: When the doors are thrown open to the garden and a charcoal-scented breeze is wafting in from the grill. Friends knocking at the door with armloads of pork and chiles and cheeses and recipes they're just itching to try. Corks popping, an endless playlist on the stereo, pans heating up. That's real cooking; that's when it's fun.

For me, the kitchen is the most special room in the house, and it's a place for adventure—not drudgery, but discovery, sharing and showing off with friends, trying new ideas. Every recipe in this book, from the simplest baked rice to a tongue-sizzling Thai curry, contains a tip, a trick, or an epiphany, something that has enriched my understanding of and love for the kitchen—and that will enrich yours, too.

Did you know, for example:

- you don't need all day to prep a spectacular cassoulet—try part of an afternoon;
- anybody can roast a duck with fall-off-the-bone meat and crispy skin;
- strawberries and tomatoes taste fantastic together on grilled bread;
- nobody makes better pickles than you do—and there's no canning required;
- toasting is not just for bread: many other foods—seeds, nuts, spices, even pastas—are immeasurably transformed with a bit of browning;
- green beans are great on the grill;
- the only reason most store-bought stock improves your food is because it's contributing salt, not much meat or vegetable flavor to speak of;
- deviled eggs are fabulous brunch fare.

There's also an irresistible bunch of desserts, most of them created by my sweet-toothed partner, Barry Rice, that you and your guests are guaranteed to inhale: Butterscotch Pots de Crème with Scotched Pecans, Chocolate–Sour Cream Layer Cake, Salted Caramel Ice Cream, or Elderflower Sabayon with Seasonal Berries, anyone?

At its heart, what I hope this book will help you do is redefine cooking as a joy rather than a burden, an opportunity to express creativity, generosity, and love.

I'm sure the most satisfying moment for many cooks comes when they present that glorious crown roast of lamb to their astonished guests. But not for me. It's back at the very beginning of the cooking day, when olive oil splashes into a shiny pan, followed by a dice of onion, carrot, and celery—three workaday vegetables, about to become heavenly soffritto, scenting the kitchen with the promise of great flavors to come. Every single time, I lean in, inches over the pan, wave the aromas into my face, and breathe in greedy snorts— one of so, so many pleasures that are the cook's, and the cook's alone.

Sure, I love hearing the expression "Bon appétit!" But the two words I like even better: "Let's cook!"

—Ted Allen

Brooklyn, New York

Note: Brand names of products are included here and there in this book solely because I like them.

For Starters

bruschetta with strawberry and tomato salad 13

BRUSCHETTA WITH HOMEMADE RICOTTA, PROSCIUTTO, AND ARUGULA 14

refrigerator pickles: cauliflower, carrots, cukes, you name it 16

FRESH GOAT CHEESE TARTLETS WITH SPICY GREENS AND PLUMS 19

herbed edamame canapés 22

ITALIAN SASHIMI: CRUDO ON THE HALF SHELL 23

two-bean dip with smoked paprika and cheese tortilla chips 24

Bruschetta WITH STRAWBERRY AND TOMATO SALAD MAKES 10 TO 15 HORS D'OEUVRES

YEP—STRAWBERRIES AND TOMATOES. I love serving this to people who don't know what's coming. They scratch their heads, expecting bruschetta to be topped with tomatoes, but what's that other familiar flavor? They always love it. Consider: tomatoes and strawberries are both sweet, tangy, and juicy. They're both fruits. They're even both red. The more I think about it, the more I want to try this on top of pasta. . . . For now, though, the combo makes a perfect summer appetizer.

1 cup diced fresh ripe strawberries

1 cup diced grape tomatoes

1 small garlic clove, minced

3 tablespoons thinly sliced basil leaves

2 tablespoons extra-virgin olive oil, plus more for brushing

2 teaspoons balsamic vinegar

½ teaspoon kosher salt

¼ teaspoon freshly ground black pepper

1 baguette, sliced on the diagonal ½ inch thick

1 In a medium bowl, combine the strawberries, tomatoes, garlic, basil, olive oil, balsamic vinegar, salt, and pepper. Let rest for 30 minutes, stirring now and then.

2 Heat an outdoor or indoor grill or grill pan to medium-high. Spread out the sliced bread on a baking sheet and brush with olive oil. Transfer to the grill, and toast the bread until golden all over, 2 or 3 minutes per side. Arrange on a platter.

3 Cover the warm grilled bread slices with a generous layer of strawberry-tomato salad. Serve immediately.

Lots of people, even fancy food-industry people, aren't sure how to pronounce the word *bruschetta*: it's brew-SKET-tuh.

Bruschetta WITH HOMEMADE RICOTTA, PROSCIUTTO, AND ARUGULA MAKES 10 TO 15 HORS D'OEUVRES

EVERY SATURDAY DURING spring, summer, and fall, Barry and I walk over for lunch at the Brooklyn Flea in Fort Greene—part antiques market, part junk sale, part craft fair, part artisanal food court. It's also great people-watching; aside from a reliably cute crew of scruffy Brooklynites and international tourists, celebs ranging from Martha Stewart to Michael Stipe are regularly spotted poking through the treasures. But the real action for us is in the well-curated street food: fabulous Salvadoran *pupusas* (thick corn tortillas stuffed with pork, beans, and cheese), brick-oven pizza, sandwiches of brisket and porchetta, and my favorite, approximated here, from Brooklyn's own Salvatore Ricotta. This is a quick and perfect treat, an ideal use for homemade ricotta.

1 baguette, sliced on the diagonal ½ inch thick

Extra-virgin olive oil, for brushing

1 garlic clove, peeled and cut in half

1 cup fresh ricotta, homemade (recipe follows) or store-bought

15 arugula leaves

¼ pound very thinly sliced prosciutto or other salty, cured pork meat, such as coppa, *lomo,* or speck

Best-quality extra-virgin olive oil, for drizzling

1 Heat an outdoor or indoor grill or grill pan to medium-high. Spread out the sliced bread on a baking sheet and brush with olive oil. Grill the bread until golden all over, 2 or 3 minutes per side. Rub one side of each piece of bread with the garlic. Arrange the bread on a platter.

2 Spread a tablespoon or two of ricotta on each piece of bread, and then press an arugula leaf into the cheese. Place a slice of prosciutto on top, drizzle with your best olive oil, and serve.

Homemade Ricotta Cheese MAKES 1½ CUPS

THERE ARE CERTAIN fresh cheeses that really taste better when you get them the day they are made, and when they've never felt the taste-killing chill of refrigeration—queso fresco, *burrata,* and fresh mozzarella come to mind. Another is ricotta, which also happens to be as easy to make as a bowl of oatmeal (well, almost), and requires no equipment more special than a thermometer and some cheesecloth. For a lasagna, where the ricotta is competing for attention with many other powerful flavors, I wouldn't bother. But for recipes that really showcase this sweet, spreadable delight—like the bruschetta on the opposite page—here's a guide to the best ricotta you will ever taste: your own.

½ gallon whole milk

2 cups buttermilk

½ teaspoon kosher salt

For this recipe, where the flavor of the milk is so important, use the highest quality you can find. Your best bet is a local dairy that is likely to pasteurize its milk more gently than a factory brand, and steer clear entirely of homogenization. For me in New York, that's Ronnybrook, which is available at many farmers' markets and better supermarkets, and hails from just a couple of hours north of the city.

1 Line a colander with 4 layers of cheesecloth, and secure it with 3 or 4 clothespins. Set the colander inside a bowl.

2 In a large saucepan over medium-high heat, with a thermometer handy, combine the whole milk and buttermilk and heat, stirring nearly constantly, until the temperature reaches 180°F. When you reach 170 to 175°F, you'll start to see fine, little curds separating from the whey. At 180°F, turn off the heat, and skim the curds from the whey using a finely slotted spoon, dropping the curds into the cheesecloth-lined colander. (Save the whey for another use, such as breadmaking.) Gather the cheesecloth around the curds and tie it with a 2-foot length of string. Gently squeeze to remove more, but not all, liquid from the cheese, and then hang over the sink or a bowl for 20 to 30 minutes to drain a bit more. (I use the string to tie the bag to my faucet.)

3 Remove the ricotta from the cheesecloth, spoon it into a container, and stir in the salt. Serve asap, preferably without refrigerating.

Refrigerator Pickles: CAULIFLOWER, CARROTS, CUKES, YOU NAME IT MAKES 2 QUARTS

I'M AS EXCITED about this recipe as anything else I've cooked in years. I love almost anything pickled!

A while back, I chose Brooklyn-based McClure's Pickles for an episode of Food Network's *The Best Thing I Ever Ate,* and I certainly stand by that call—McClure's spears are big, crispy, and perfectly spiced. Unfortunately, they are also twelve dollars a jar. Now, I understand that costs are higher for small, artisanal food-makers, whom I will always love and support. But for pennies you can make great pickles at home— easily, satisfyingly, and, if you wish, organically—and you don't have to do any canning or fermenting.

How? Fresh refrigerator pickles. No sterilizing, no precooking the veggies, no piping hot jars. And no need to make sixty-seven cases of the stuff; you're not doing this under pressure to preserve a giant crop from the garden, as your granny was, but just because you want two jars of great pickles. This light brine works great with many foods: cucumbers, of course, but also carrots, turnips, onions, green beans, asparagus, jalapeños, watermelon rind, unripe green tomatoes, even apples. And your pickles will last for weeks in the fridge (where you *must* store them at all times).

BRINE

10 garlic cloves, peeled

2 cups white vinegar

6 teaspoons kosher salt

Several sprigs of fresh dill

1 teaspoon celery seed

1 teaspoon coriander seed

1 teaspoon mustard seed

½ teaspoon black peppercorns

½ teaspoon pink pepper-corns (if you have 'em)

VEGETABLES

6 Kirby cucumbers, quartered lengthwise

6 medium carrots, peeled and cut in half lengthwise

A handful of green beans

A few pieces of cauliflower to tuck wherever they'll fit

4 small hot red chiles or 2 jalapeños

(recipe continues)

Simmering the garlic in water cooks out sulfur compounds that otherwise will cause the cloves to turn a harmless but very unappetizing blue-green color from the acid in the vinegar.

Keep the chiles whole for mild heat. Halve them for a spicier kick.

A canning funnel with a wide spout is helpful for pouring the hot brine into the jars; a regular funnel is your next-best option. Otherwise, transfer hot brine from the pan to a pitcher before attempting to pour. Trust me on this.

1 In a medium saucepan, bring 4 cups water to a boil, reduce the heat so the water simmers, and add the garlic. Cook for 5 minutes. Add the vinegar and salt, raise the heat, and bring to a boil, stirring until the salt dissolves. Remove from the heat.

2 In 2 clean, 1-quart mason jars, place a few sprigs of dill. Divide the seeds and peppercorns between the jars. Using tongs, remove the garlic from the brine and place 5 cloves in each jar. Then pack the jars full of cucumbers, carrots, beans, cauliflower, and chiles. You want them to be tightly stuffed.

3 Bring the brine back to a boil, pour it over the vegetables to cover completely, let cool, and refrigerate. The pickles will taste good in just a few hours, better after a couple of days. And they'll keep for about 3 months.

Fresh Goat Cheese Tartlets

WITH SPICY GREENS AND PLUMS SERVES 4

WHEN YOU'RE COOKING for lunch or brunch, as opposed to dinner, the calculus is somehow different. Portions are smaller and entrées are often salad-based; yet it feels right to have rich elements, such as pastry, with quiches and tarts. You want the food to look a bit elegant, suggesting composed plates. Here's your dish, which tames the tang of goat cheese just a little and brings out its sweetness with freshly grated nutmeg. Another nice thing about this recipe: because these little tarts are assembled and baked in a muffin tin, they're beautifully portable as a "covered dish"; pack 'em up and bake them in your host's oven (ask permission beforehand to make sure the oven's not taken—or broken).

TART DOUGH

1½ cups all-purpose flour, plus more for rolling

1 teaspoon baking powder

¾ teaspoon table salt

6 tablespoons unsalted butter, cut into small pieces, cold

1 large egg

3 tablespoons heavy cream, or more if needed

GOAT CHEESE FILLING

1 cup fresh goat cheese

2 large eggs

½ cup heavy cream

2 tablespoons chopped flat-leaf parsley leaves

¼ teaspoon freshly grated nutmeg

½ teaspoon kosher salt

Freshly ground black pepper

SALAD

6 cups spicy greens, such as mustard greens, arugula, or watercress

8 plums, halved, pitted, and sliced into 6 wedges each

2 tablespoons red wine vinegar

¼ cup best-quality extra-virgin olive oil

Kosher salt and freshly ground black pepper

1 Preheat the oven to 350°F.

2 Make the tart dough: Sift the flour, baking powder, and table salt into a mixing bowl. Add the butter and cut it into the flour using your fingers, a fork, or a pastry cutter until it resembles coarse meal. Add the egg and cream, and mix to combine. If the dough seems dry, add a bit more cream. Press into a circle, wrap with plastic, and place in the fridge for at least 30 minutes or up to overnight.

(recipe continues)

Use a Microplane grater—a must-have tool often used for grating citrus—for the nutmeg. And speaking of citrus, Jeff Mosher, executive chef at the Robert Mondavi Winery, showed me during a recent cooking demo a better way to grate its zest with a Microplane: hold the fruit in one hand, the grater in the other, on top, teeth down, and grate the top of the citrus. That way, you can see where you've grated and where you haven't.

3 Make the goat cheese filling: In a bowl, mix together the cheese, eggs, cream, parsley, nutmeg, salt, and pepper.

4 Remove the dough from the fridge. On a lightly floured surface, roll out the dough to $1/4$-inch thickness, and cut into 3-inch circles. Press into the cups of a 12-count muffin tin. Reroll scraps and cut if needed to fill all the cups. Scoop $1/3$ cup of the filling into each crust and place in the oven. Bake for 25 to 30 minutes, until puffed and golden brown. Remove from the oven and let cool.

5 In a bowl, toss the greens, plums, vinegar, and oil. Season with salt and pepper. Serve the salad alongside the tarts.

HERBED Edamame Canapés

THIS JUST IN: There are other things you can do with edamame besides boiling them for four minutes and salting them. I actually originally conceived this recipe for fava beans, a delightful vegetable—except when out of season, or, more pointedly, when you are the poor prep cook who has to shell the things. You can get the same result, year-round, with bags of frozen, shelled soybeans, which make a vibrant spread for vegetables or toast.

1½ teaspoons kosher salt

½ pound frozen, shelled edamame (soybeans), thawed

1 teaspoon unsalted butter

2 large shallots, halved and sliced into thin half moons

¼ teaspoon freshly ground black pepper

1 small garlic clove, smashed and peeled

3 tablespoons fresh ricotta, homemade (page 15) or store-bought

2 tablespoons extra-virgin olive oil

½ teaspoon grated lemon zest

1 tablespoon fresh lemon juice

1 tablespoon chopped tarragon leaves

Endive leaves, cucumber or jicama slices, or toasted baguette slices

1 Put a medium saucepan half full of water over high heat and bring to a boil. Add 1 teaspoon of the salt and the edamame, bring the water back to a boil, and cook for 1 minute. Drain and transfer to a bowl filled with ice water to stop cooking. Once cool, drain well.

2 Melt the butter in a medium skillet over medium heat. Add the shallots and cook, stirring occasionally, until golden brown, about 7 minutes. Season with the remaining ½ teaspoon salt and the pepper.

3 Combine the edamame, shallots, garlic, ricotta cheese, olive oil, lemon zest, and juice in the bowl of a food processor and pulse to make a thick, slightly chunky puree. Season with salt and pepper. Scrape the mixture into a bowl and mix in the chopped tarragon. Spoon onto endive leaves, cucumber slices, toasts, or what-have-you, and serve.

Italian Sashimi:
CRUDO ON THE HALF SHELL   MAKES 16 HORS D'OEUVRES

ACTUALLY, whether this so-called Italian sashimi is served in a shell—or at all—*must* depend entirely on the freshness of shellfish (or fish) available to you. This is a raw seafood dish, one not even "cured" over time in citrus juice the way ceviche is. I went to the market looking for littleneck clams and fish, and ended up substituting sea scallops for the latter because they were fresher.

4 sea scallops

16 littleneck clams

4 teaspoons fresh lemon juice

4 teaspoons best-quality extra-virgin olive oil

1 teaspoon minced jalapeño pepper

Coarse sea salt

1 Wrap the scallops in plastic wrap or put them in a zipper bag, making sure that they are not touching, and freeze for 1 hour. Cut the scallops into ¼-inch dice.

2 Rinse the clams under cold water to remove grit. Using an oyster shucker, shuck the clams, being careful not to mingle shell fragments with meat. Wash 16 half shells very well and reserve. Chop the meat coarsely.

3 In a medium bowl, toss both shellfish with the lemon juice, olive oil, and jalapeño. Spoon into the reserved clam shells. Top with a sprinkle of coarse salt. Serve immediately.

I like the floral flavor of Meyer lemons and use their juice in this recipe whenever they are in season.

See notes on buying scallops on page 164. Freezing the scallops briefly makes them slightly firmer and easier to dice.

Two-Bean Dip WITH SMOKED PAPRIKA AND CHEESE TORTILLA CHIPS MAKES ABOUT 4 CUPS

YOU CAN CHOOSE to simplify this recipe by cooking both the white and black beans together, or by going with only white, or only black. But why would you? This is an easy way to get a great-looking presentation with a simple dip, taking it to a higher level of style. You also could choose to use chipotles with only the black beans, leaving the white-bean side subtle and mild. And while you could just serve store-bought tortilla chips alongside, for better flavor and texture, make fresh chips yourself—and from flour tortillas instead of corn. It's easy. It's worth it.

3 slices thick-cut bacon

1 medium red onion, chopped

1 yellow bell pepper, cored, seeded, and chopped

1 teaspoon chili powder

½ teaspoon ground cumin

½ teaspoon dried oregano

2 teaspoons chopped canned chipotle chiles in adobo sauce

1 (15-ounce) can black beans, rinsed and drained

1 cup chicken stock, preferably homemade (page 173) or low-sodium store-bought

1 (15-ounce) can white cannellini beans, rinsed and drained

Kosher salt and freshly ground black pepper

½ cup sour cream

3 tablespoons chopped cilantro leaves

1   In a skillet, cook the bacon over medium heat until crisp, about 5 minutes. Put the bacon on a cutting board, coarsely chop, and set aside.

2   Remove all but 1 tablespoon bacon drippings from the pan. Sauté the onion and bell pepper until soft, about 6 minutes. Add the chili powder, cumin, and oregano, and cook until fragrant, about 1 minute.

3   Divide the onion mixture in half and scoop one-half into a second skillet. Divide the chipotle chiles between the skillets. Add the black beans, with half of the chicken stock, to one skillet, and the white beans, with the remaining stock, to the other. Simmer both mixtures over medium-low heat, stirring now and then, for 5 minutes.

4   Scoop 1 cup of the white bean mixture into a food processor, and puree until smooth. Mix back into the cooked white beans. Repeat this step with the black beans, keeping the black and white mixtures separate. Season each mixture with salt and pepper, and refrigerate in separate bowls, covered, for 2 hours.

5   Divide the bacon between the bowls and stir it into the bean mixtures. In a shallow presentation bowl, spoon the white bean dip into one side and the black bean dip into the other. Using a large spoon, swirl the black beans

(recipe continues)

about halfway around the edge of the bowl into the white beans, and, with a clean spoon, do the same with the white beans in the same direction—making two interlocking comma shapes in the bowl (or a yin and yang symbol). Spoon half of the sour cream into the fat part of each "comma," sprinkle equal parts cilantro over each dollop, and serve.

Baked Smoked Paprika and Cheese Tortilla Chips MAKES 6 DOZEN CHIPS

FRESH, CRISPY, and made with real cheese—so much better than chips from a bag.

6 (6-inch) flour tortillas

4 ounces sharp Cheddar cheese, finely grated (1 cup)

½ teaspoon smoked spicy paprika

1 large egg white

1 Preheat the oven to 350°F.

2 Stack the tortillas, cut in half, and then cut each half into 6 wedges. Arrange the tortilla wedges in a single layer on a baking sheet. In a small bowl, mix together the cheese and smoked paprika. Using a brush, lightly brush the chips with the egg white and then sprinkle with the cheese mixture. Bake for 12 minutes, until golden and crispy. Let cool before serving.

FIVE-SPICE **Holiday Nuts** MAKES 2 CUPS

HERE, THE POWER of texture meets the virtues of toasting spices multiplied by the excitement of pairing sweetness with savory—*and* the endorphin-producing power of spicy heat. In a bowl or on a salad, these babies always steal the show. They are a great showcase for Chinese five-spice powder—a mixture of cinnamon, powdered cassia buds, star anise, ginger, and cloves.

2 tablespoons extra-virgin olive oil, plus more for the pan

1 teaspoon Chinese five-spice powder

½ teaspoon curry powder

¼ teaspoon cayenne pepper

2 tablespoons sugar

2 cups mixed nuts, such as walnuts, hazelnuts, almonds, pecans, or cashews

1 teaspoon kosher salt

1 Line a baking sheet with parchment paper and lightly oil the paper. Heat the 2 tablespoons oil in a large nonstick sauté pan over medium heat. Add the five-spice powder, curry, and cayenne, and cook until fragrant, about 10 seconds. Stir in the sugar and then the nuts. Stir until the mixture is light golden brown and the nuts are completely coated, about 5 minutes.

2 Spoon the mixture onto the prepared baking sheet, separating the nuts with a spoon. Sprinkle with the salt, and let cool. Store in an airtight container for up to 1 week.

I use kosher salt throughout this book because I like its coarse-milled texture. If you're using regular, fine-milled table salt, use about 20 percent less.

ANYONE-CAN-MAKE Great Crusty Baguettes MAKES 2 MEDIUM BAGUETTES

PROBABLY THE MOST gorgeous bread I've ever baked is the breakthrough, no-knead recipe invented by Sullivan Street Bakery owner Jim Lahey (you can find it online). It turned me into a bread baker, and I will never go back—but the dough has to rise overnight, and I don't always plan that far ahead. When I need fresh bread *today,* I turn to this recipe. I like the heartiness of whole grains, so I use a little whole-wheat flour, but you can certainly go with straight-up white flour, if you prefer. Do try to get your hands on bread flour, if at all possible; the high protein content makes for the best chewiness and crust.

3¼ cups bread flour, plus more for kneading

¼ cup whole-wheat flour

2¼ teaspoons kosher salt

1 teaspoon active dry yeast

1½ cups warm water

2 tablespoons extra-virgin olive oil

Cornmeal, for dusting

1 large egg

Note that you'll need a food processor, pizza stone, and clean spray bottle filled with fresh water for this recipe.

This bread takes only a few minutes of active work, but needs about 5 hours of rising, plus about 30 minutes to bake. So if dinner's at 7:00, get started by 1:00.

1 Put the bread flour, whole-wheat flour, salt, and yeast in the food processor, and mix for a few seconds. Then, with the blade running, add the water and 1 tablespoon of the oil. Run the machine for 30 seconds; the dough should form a sticky ball that spins around inside the bowl. Rub the inside of a large bowl with the remaining tablespoon of olive oil, add the dough, and turn to coat. Cover the bowl with plastic wrap or a damp towel, and allow the dough to rise in a warm place until doubled in size, about 3 hours.

2 Lightly flour your hands and a countertop; then, scoop the dough—which will be very sticky—onto it. Cut the dough in half and shape each half into a rectangle. Let rest, covered with a damp cloth, for about 30 minutes, to allow the dough to relax and become supple.

3 Lightly dust a cutting board or pizza peel with cornmeal. On the countertop, arrange the long side of one dough rectangle facing you. Fold the dough lengthwise halfway onto itself from the edge closest to you, then fold in the edge farthest from you to completely cover the first fold, forming a thinner

(recipe continues)

rectangle, and pinch the seam. Roll into a baguette shape about 2 inches thick, place on one half of the cornmeal-dusted board, seam side down, and shake the board to make sure you'll be able to slide the dough off and onto the pizza stone later. Repeat with the second piece of dough, placing it on the other half of the board, at least 3 inches apart from the first. Let rise, covered with a damp cloth, for 1 to 2 hours.

4 Put a pizza stone in the oven, set the temperature to 450°F, and preheat for a solid 30 minutes. This is important to fully heat the stone.

If you like, add to the dough a tablespoon of fresh herbs, poppy seeds, or chopped almonds. Even subtle additions, such as a few grinds of white pepper, contribute interesting new flavors.

Make the herb butter that goes with Herbed Roast Chicken with Charred Poblano Sauce (page 114), and smear it all over this bread while the bread is still warm from the oven. Yes—do that.

5 Meanwhile, whip the egg in a small bowl with 1 tablespoon water, and then lightly brush the egg wash onto both loaves. Using a sharp, serrated knife, make 3 or 4 diagonal slashes across the top of each loaf.

6 Slide the dough from the board onto the hot pizza stone, using a swift jerking action and making sure the loaves are perpendicular to the stone. Quickly spray the loaves and the inside of the oven with water from the spray bottle several times. After 5 minutes, spray inside the oven again. Bake the baguettes until golden brown, 20 to 25 minutes. Cool on a wire rack. Eat or freeze the day you bake.

ON PREHEATING PANS AND OVENS

Every now and then, you'll come upon recipes that tell you preheating the oven is unnecessary. These recipes are wrong.

HERE'S THE THING:

A lot of food is best cooked at high heat: pizzeria ovens are often set at 750 to 1,000°F, while some steakhouses heat their broilers to 1,300°F to get a thick char on rare meat. Home ovens max out at 500°F, so you're already at a disadvantage compared to restaurant chefs. And I don't care how powerful your oven is; it's not going from 0 to 500 instantly, or in 5 minutes, and isn't even that hot when the temperature indicator light goes off. All that tells you is that the *air* inside the oven has reached temperature; the metal surfaces have not, nor, certainly, has your inch-thick ceramic pizza stone. And the air will escape the second you open the door to put your cold food inside it (further dragging things down), and it will take time to reheat. For some high-temperature recipes, I preheat my oven for a solid 30 minutes, and I'm a big believer in this.

SIMILARLY IMPORTANT . . .

Getting your pans to temperature. Browning food is one of the most important ways to create flavor, and you need hot pans for a successful sear. But just as important: not tearing your food to pieces in the process. Letting your pan get good and hot first and only *then* adding your oil and protein—a technique some call Hot Pan, Cold Oil—keeps food from sticking. Try it. The minute you put food in the pan, give the pan a strong shake to assure the food slides around; then wait a few seconds, and give it another shake to make sure it's still loose. That hard sear makes your food less sticky, unable any longer to bond to the pan. You're good to go.

Of course I appreciate the impulse to conserve energy. But if you're ruining food, you're not saving anything.

White Bean Soup Shooters

WITH A BIT OF BACON MAKES 16 SHOTS OR 4 SMALL BOWLS

IT'S NO SECRET to caterers, but most home cooks probably don't realize that soup makes great cocktail-party food—all you need are shot glasses. It's warming, welcoming, cheap (well, unless you're using lobster and truffles), and easy. Collecting mix-and-match shooters makes for an excellent flea-market mission.

This soup is a Tuscan classic, made simple. The addition of a teeny bit of bacon lends a slight smoky-salty richness and a bit of crunch.

3 (½-inch-thick) slices crusty bread from a baguette, toasted

Fresh goat cheese

2 slices bacon, diced

1 tablespoon extra-virgin olive oil

1 tablespoon unsalted butter

2 shallots, chopped

3 garlic cloves, coarsely chopped

2 (15-ounce cans) cannellini or other white beans, rinsed and drained

1½ cups chicken stock, preferably homemade (page 173), or low-sodium store-bought

6 sage leaves, chopped

⅓ cup heavy cream

1 teaspoon fresh lemon juice

½ teaspoon kosher salt, or to taste

¼ teaspoon cayenne, or to taste

1 Smear the toast generously with goat cheese, and cut into ¾-inch croutons. Set aside.

2 In a medium saucepan, fry the bacon over medium-low heat until halfway done, about 5 minutes. Add the oil, butter, and shallots, and sauté until soft, about 6 minutes. Add the garlic and cook until fragrant, 1 minute. Add the beans, chicken stock, and sage, bring to a simmer, and cook for 15 minutes.

3 Using a blender or food processor, puree in batches (and be careful; hot liquids are prone to explode when whipped!). Return the pureed soup to the pan, and add the cream, lemon juice, salt, and cayenne.

4 Ladle into shot glasses, top with croutons, and serve immediately.

Bourbon Squash Soup

I DON'T DRINK MUCH WHISKEY, but I love to cook with it. Bourbon, in particular, has so much sweetness and smoke, and the alcohol seems to breathe depth into the aromas of whatever's cooking. All those attributes really shine with pumpkin, as well as other squashes, such as acorn or butternut, and also sweet potatoes and yams. Add my favorite, catch-all garnish, the baked Parmesan cheese crisp known as frico, with a twist—hulled, toasted pumpkin seeds, aka pepitas—and you've really stirred up a winner.

SOUP

- 2 tablespoons extra-virgin olive oil, plus more for brushing
- 1 acorn or butternut squash, halved and seeded
- Kosher salt and freshly ground black pepper
- 1 medium yellow onion, chopped
- 2 celery ribs, chopped
- 2 medium carrots, chopped
- ½ hot red chile, seeded and chopped
- 2 garlic cloves, chopped
- 2 teaspoons fresh thyme leaves or 1 teaspoon dried
- ¼ cup bourbon whiskey, such as Maker's Mark
- 4 cups chicken stock, preferably homemade (page 173), or low-sodium store-bought

FRICO

- 1 cup freshly grated Parmesan cheese
- 2 teaspoons all-purpose flour
- 2 tablespoons pepitas (shelled pumpkin seeds)
- 1 teaspoon finely chopped rosemary or thyme leaves (optional)
- A grind of black pepper (optional)
- ¼ teaspoon cayenne (optional)

For the record, the old saw that all the alcohol cooks away with heat is not 100 percent true; however, a good percentage of it does, plus, you're starting here with a tiny amount—no one's going to fail a breathalyzer because of this.

If you want to forgo the frico, you can simply garnish this soup with toasted pumpkin seeds, crème fraîche, and bacon bits. But I'm telling you, a fresh-baked parm cracker is amazing.

1 Make the soup: Preheat the oven to 375°F.

2 Brush olive oil on the cut sides of the squash and season with salt. Put the squash cut side down on a baking sheet, cover with foil, and roast for 1 hour, until tender. Remove from the oven, turn the squash over, and let cool. Scoop the squash out of the rind and set aside the flesh.

3 Lower the oven temperature to 350°F.

4 In a large Dutch oven or stockpot over medium heat, warm the olive oil, then add the onion, celery, and carrots, and cook until soft, 8 minutes. Add the chile, garlic, and thyme, and cook until fragrant, 1 minute. Then, add the squash, whiskey, stock, 1 teaspoon salt, and 1/2 teaspoon pepper, and bring to a boil. Reduce the heat and simmer until slightly thickened, 20 minutes.

5 Meanwhile, make the frico: Mix together in a small bowl the Parmesan, flour, pepitas, and any of the optional add-ins. On a baking sheet lined with parchment paper, make 1-tablespoon piles of the mixture with a couple inches between each, and spread them out into ovals about 4 inches long and 2 wide. Bake in the oven until golden brown, 6 to 8 minutes. Let cool on the baking sheet.

6 If you have time, first allow the soup to cool, and then puree in batches or with an immersion blender, reheat before serving. If not, be aware that hot liquids can explode out of food processors and blenders; hold on to the lid with a kitchen towel and proceed carefully. Season to taste with salt and pepper.

7 Tuck a frico into each bowl of hot soup, and serve.

KILL YOUR TUPPERWARE

I believe that for a serious home cook, the freezer could be the second-most important tool in the kitchen. (My chef's knife is number one, of course.) There is no better device for making cooking easy and efficient. Making soup? Make extra. Ditto lasagna. Stew. Stock. Soffritto. But here's what really revolutionized my use of the chilly box: restaurant takeout containers.

The curries and saag paneer we order from our neighborhood Indian place come in sturdy, clear, plastic pint containers that seem a shame to throw into landfills. So I started washing them and using them for storage. Instantly, I was hooked—and almost as instantly, I had used them all and needed more.

Please stay with me, here—this is exciting stuff!

For many years, I froze food in zipper bags. Advantage: I could flatten liquids in the bag, enabling me later to snap off only the amount I needed. Disadvantages: Once frozen, the bags became icy, irregularly shaped, sharp-edged missiles that routinely slipped off the shelf and onto my big toe. Plus, they got torn; they didn't stack or label well, so I could never find anything; they were only good for a single use; they reduced air circulation in the freezer . . . you get the idea.

Plastic pint containers are the perfect size for one or two portions of pretty much anything. They freeze and thaw quickly, they stack gorgeously in the freezer, cold air easily moves around them, and they're dishwasher- and microwave-safe. Also, they're dirt cheap. The only problem is finding a restaurant-supply place that will sell you fewer than five thousand of them. Find a store in your town, and sweet-talk. If they won't help you, call The Brooklyn Kitchen (718-389-2982), ask for Taylor or Harry, and tell them I sent you.

P.S. For an additional touch of elegance, invest in a label maker; I use a P-touch from Brother. Labels are easy to attach, and just as easy to remove. Or do what chefs do: write on masking tape with a marker.

Devilish Eggs WITH CHEDDAR, CHIPOTLE, AND CHIVES MAKES 24 HALVES

BECAUSE THERE IS no happier food than a deviled egg. Because chipotle peppers—that is, smoked jalapeños canned in fiery barbecue sauce called adobo—taste so good with egg, Cheddar, and chives. And because I need to share with you this crucial technique: the moment you're done boiling your eggs, plunge them into an ice bath. This prevents that ugly, moldy-looking green edge you otherwise often get around the yolks. Eggcellent.

1 dozen large eggs

½ cup finely shredded Cheddar cheese

¼ cup mayonnaise

¼ cup sour cream

2 tablespoons chopped chives

4 teaspoons chopped canned chipotle chiles in adobo sauce, or more to taste

½ teaspoon sweet paprika

Pinch of kosher salt

1 Put the eggs in a saucepan, cover with cold water by 1 inch, and bring to a boil over high heat. Reduce the heat and simmer for 10 minutes; then drain and immediately plunge the eggs into an ice bath to cool.

2 Peel the eggs, slice in half lengthwise, and scoop out the yolks. Put the whites on a platter. Pass the yolks through a sieve into a medium bowl, or just mash with a fork. Mix in the cheese, mayo, sour cream, chives (reserving 1 teaspoon for garnish), chipotles, paprika, and salt.

3 Use a pastry bag fitted with a ½-inch tip to pipe the filling into the whites, or, if you're less fancy, use 2 spoons. Sprinkle with the reserved chives. Cover loosely with plastic wrap and refrigerate until serving, which should be within a day.

BRUNCHY DEVILED EGGS WITH SMOKED SALMON AND CAVIAR MAKES 24 HALVES

Everybody loves deviled eggs; there are rarely leftovers. So why reserve them for picnics and holidays? Here's a version that cries out for a brunch buffet. The caviar is just a luxurious touch; you'll have a delightfully flavorful egg with or without it.

Cook and prepare 12 eggs as for Devilish Eggs with Cheddar, Chipotle, and Chives, mixing in 2 tablespoons mayonnaise, 2 tablespoons sour cream, 2 tablespoons extra-virgin olive oil, 1 tablespoon Dijon mustard, 1 heaping tablespoon minced shallot, 2 tablespoons minced drained capers, and 1 ounce minced smoked salmon. Garnish with 1 ounce minced smoked salmon and 1 ounce sturgeon caviar or salmon roe.

NOT EXACTLY CHINESE **Pork Buns** MAKES 32 BUNS

THERE IS NO ITEM more popular at dim sum than *char siu bao*, the slightly sweet Chinese buns stuffed with long-cooked pork and steamed to fluffy, spongy yumminess. And, having finished the exercise of developing pulled-pork recipes in three different vocabularies—American Southern, Mexican, and Indian—it occurred to me that all three of those preparations would be just as fantastic in a steamed pillow of dough as the original Cantonese with hoisin sauce, each with its own appropriate sauce or accompaniment. Upon further investigation: they are. This dish is a bit of work, but as long as you give the dough enough time to rise and become soft, it's fairly easy. The second time, you can do it with your eyes closed.

¼ cup warm water

1 package active dry yeast

½ cup sugar

4 cups all-purpose flour, plus more for kneading and rolling

½ teaspoon baking powder

½ teaspoon table salt

2 tablespoons vegetable shortening, plus more for bowl

1 cup plus 1 tablespoon warm whole milk

2 cups cooked North Carolina Pulled Pork (page 189), Pork Vindaloo (page 192), or Pork and Black Bean Tinga (page 191)

Condiment based on pork recipe (see below)

1 In a small bowl, combine the warm water, yeast, and a pinch of the sugar and let sit for 5 minutes, until foamy.

2 Put the flour, baking powder, salt, and remaining sugar in the bowl of a food processor, and pulse to blend. Add the shortening and pulse a few more times. Turn the processor on to its continuous mode, and, through the feed tube, add the yeast mixture and then the milk. Continue processing. As the flour absorbs the liquid, after about a minute, the dough should form a ball. Turn the dough out onto a lightly floured surface, and knead just until smooth. Put the dough in an oiled bowl, turn to coat, cover with plastic wrap, and put in a warm spot until doubled in size, about an hour.

3 Meanwhile, put the pork in a strainer set over a bowl to drain off some of its liquid.

You'll need a food processor, parchment paper, and some kind of steamer; Chinese cooks use bamboo models, but steel is fine, too.

(recipe continues)

4 Turn the dough out onto a floured surface and roll into a long, fat rope. Cut into 4 equal pieces, roll those into ropes; then, cut each into 8 pieces. Drape a damp, clean kitchen towel over the dough pieces and let them rest for a few minutes.

5 Cut 8 (3-inch) squares of parchment paper. Roll each piece of dough into a ball and press into a disk. With a rolling pin, flatten to a thin, 5-inch circle. Place a scant tablespoon of pork in the center of each disk. Gather the dough up around the filling to form a purse, pressing the dough together and twisting to seal the top. Set each bun on a parchment square. Cover the buns with a damp kitchen towel, and let rise for another 30 minutes.

6 Fill a steamer with water, cover it, and heat over high heat to produce a strong, rolling boil. Steam the buns (on their parchment squares) for 15 minutes and serve immediately with the appropriate condiment, below:

For North Carolina Pulled Pork, make Pickled Red Onions (page 190).

For Pork Vindaloo, stir ½ cup chopped cucumber and 1 tablespoon chopped dill into 1 cup plain yogurt.

For Pork and Black Bean Tinga, make guacamole. Mash 1 ripe Hass avocado, add the juice of 1 lime, ½ teaspoon table salt, 1 minced small garlic clove, 1 tablespoon chopped cilantro leaves, and ½ ripe tomato, diced.

Thai-Grilled Beef Skewers
WITH PICKLED CUCUMBERS   SERVES 4 TO 6 AS AN APPETIZER

THERE IS JUST no easier way to pack delicious flavor into food than to give it a quick soak in soy sauce, garlic, ginger, sesame, and lime. Beef, fish, chicken, shrimp, vegetables, tofu, noodles, two-by-fours—try to think of anything that isn't instantly made delicious with these flavors, and even more so when a grill is part of the equation. Another reason I wanted this snack in the collection: when you're cooking at home, for friends—as opposed to eating at a neighborhood joint that's worried about its food cost—you can cook a dish like this with a quality cut, such as rib eye or sirloin. That really makes this a treat, especially when paired with *ajad,* the classic Thai satay condiment of sweet-and-sour–dressed cucumbers and chiles. And finally, of course, as *Chopped* judge Chris Santos is fond of saying, everything tastes better on a stick.

PICKLED CUCUMBERS

¼ cup sugar

½ teaspoon kosher salt

¼ cup unseasoned rice vinegar

½ Asian cucumber, peeled, halved lengthwise, seeded, and thinly sliced

1 small hot red or green chile, thinly sliced

½ cup thinly sliced red onion

¼ cup chopped cilantro leaves

BEEF SKEWERS

½ cup soy sauce

4 teaspoons rice vinegar

2 teaspoons toasted sesame oil

2 teaspoons fish sauce

2 teaspoons mirin

3 garlic cloves, finely chopped

2 teaspoons minced peeled fresh ginger

1 tablespoon packed light brown sugar

4 teaspoons sesame seeds, toasted

2 teaspoons red pepper flakes or Thai chili paste

Juice of 1 lime

1 pound sirloin, rib eye, or New York strip steak, cut into 1-inch cubes

2 scallions (white and light green parts), cut into 1-inch lengths, plus additional, sliced, for garnish

1 First, pickle the cucumbers: In a small saucepan, heat the sugar, salt, vinegar, and ¼ cup water over medium-high heat until the sugar and salt dissolve; remove from heat. Put the cucumber, chile, and red onion in a medium bowl, and pour the hot brine over. Let cool; then add the cilantro. Chill.

(recipe continues)

2 Make the beef skewers: In a medium bowl, blend the soy sauce, vinegar, sesame oil, fish sauce, mirin, garlic, ginger, brown sugar, sesame seeds, and red pepper flakes. Pour half of the mixture into a serving bowl, add the lime juice, and reserve for a dipping sauce. Put the beef cubes in a zipper bag and pour in the remaining marinade. Seal the bag and massage the marinade into the meat. Put in a bowl, and refrigerate for 1 to 4 hours.

3 Preheat a grill to high heat.

4 Drain the meat, discarding the marinade. Thread the cubes onto skewers (1 to 4 per skewer), separating each cube with a round of scallion. Grill directly over coals, turning once, until nicely charred, about 3 minutes per side.

5 Sprinkle with sliced scallions. Serve warm or cold with the reserved marinade for dipping and the pickled cucumbers and chiles on the side.

If you're using wooden skewers, soak them in water for 30 minutes to keep them from burning.

TINY **Twice-Baked Potatoes** WITH SMOKED PAPRIKA AND BACON MAKES 40 HORS D'OEUVRES

THIS IS A TEXTBOOK example of a party nibble that takes a bit of labor ahead of time but is effortless when the party is under way—which is to say, it's exactly what you want from an hors d'oeuvre. Take classic, cheesy twice-baked potatoes and shrink them to bite-size. Then, give them the always welcome yum of bacon bits (real ones, por favor). Finally, amp up the smokiness and spice with the "it" flavor from Spain, spicy smoked paprika (look for "picante" on the label).

20 small baby red potatoes (about 1 pound)

1½ tablespoons extra-virgin olive oil

Fine sea salt and freshly ground black pepper

2 slices of bacon

½ cup shredded sharp Cheddar cheese

2 tablespoons sour cream

1 scallion (green part only), minced

¼ teaspoon smoked spicy paprika

2 tablespoons unsalted butter

⅓ cup heavy cream or whole milk or a combination

1 Preheat the oven to 400°F.

2 Leaving the skins on, cut the potatoes in half crosswise, and place cut side down on a parchment-lined baking sheet. Drizzle with the olive oil, sprinkle with salt and pepper, and toss until evenly covered. Bake for 20 minutes, until cooked through. Cool completely.

3 Cook the bacon over medium-low heat until crispy, about 10 minutes. Drain on paper towels, and then mince.

4 In a bowl, combine the bacon, cheese, sour cream, scallion, paprika, ¼ teaspoon salt, and ¼ teaspoon pepper.

5 Using a sharp knife, trim a tiny slice off the round end of each potato half, so that they can stand upright. Using a melon baller or a paring knife and small spoon, carefully scoop enough potato flesh from each potato half to form little cups. Mash the scooped-out potato into the cheese mixture along with the butter and cream.

6 Spoon the mashed stuffing into a pastry bag or a freezer-strength zipper bag with a corner snipped off, and pipe it into the potato cups. Put the potatoes on a baking sheet, cover with plastic wrap, and refrigerate for up to 1 day.

7 At serving time, preheat the oven to 350°F.

8 Bake the potatoes until heated through, about 10 minutes. Serve warm.

Salads and Sides

Arugula WITH SUN-DRIED TOMATO VINAIGRETTE AND FRESH MOOTZ SERVES 4

THE WORD "FRESH" is thrown around so much by food companies these days that its true meaning can be lost—until you have an experience like this: Years ago, my friend Scott Omelianuk took me to his (as he pronounces it) Eye-talian deli, Vito's, on Washington Street in Hoboken, New Jersey, and bought a pound of mozzarella. The cheese had been made that afternoon, as it's made all day, every day, and had never been refrigerated. Eat, Scott instructed. I ate. And as many Caprese salads as I'd enjoyed in my days, never had I tasted such milky sweetness in a fresh mootz. Before flying back home to Chicago, where I lived at the time, I bought another blob of the stuff, and ate half of it on the plane. This simple salad celebrates that kind of mootz, which pairs so nicely with the tangy sweetness of dried tomatoes and the bite of arugula.

¼ cup sun-dried tomatoes

2 tablespoons red wine vinegar

1 garlic clove, peeled and quartered

½ teaspoon thyme leaves

½ teaspoon kosher salt

½ cup peppery extra-virgin olive oil

4 cups arugula

8 ounces freshest available mozzarella (do not refrigerate)

1 Chop the tomatoes coarsely and put them in a small bowl with the vinegar to rehydrate, 15 minutes. Dump the tomatoes and vinegar into the bowl of a food processor with the garlic, thyme, and salt. Run the processor and add the oil slowly in a thin stream through the feed tube to emulsify the vinaigrette.

2 In a large bowl, toss the arugula with the tomato vinaigrette. Divide the greens among 4 plates. Top with lumps of the cheese, and serve.

These days I get my mootz fix at Greene Grape Provisions in Fort Greene, Brooklyn. Seek out the freshest in your neck of the woods. (If you can't find any, bring some back from your next vacation to New York, Hoboken, or any of the number of great Little Italys across America, but remember to buy extra: some to eat on the plane and some to make this dish.)

Heirloom Gazpacho Salad WITH GRILLED BREAD AND CRAB

THE FLAVORS OF gazpacho are the perfect distillation of sunshine and heat: sweet, tangy, spicy. For me, they *are* summer. One of my favorite days of the year, by far: the day the heirloom tomatoes finally show up at my farmers' market in Brooklyn's Fort Greene Park. I buy green zebras, Italian hearts, black princes—invariably way too many—and run home to make Caprese salads, panzanellas, uncooked tomato sauce for pasta, and of course, the famous cold soup of Spain, usually slurping it down before there's any time for chilling.

Then, this past summer, I had a eureka moment (or should I say, a "D'oh!"): why was I chilling a soup made of tomatoes, which suppresses their sweetness? Why use a machine to liquefy vegetables that are at their peak flavor *and* texture? Worst, why buy expensive heirlooms and then eliminate the ability to differentiate their wildly different tastes and colors?

And so a gazpacho salad was born.

4 (1-inch-thick) diagonal slices baguette or other crusty bread

½ cup extra-virgin olive oil, plus more for brushing

3 medium garlic cloves

Kosher salt and freshly ground black pepper

2½ pounds mixed heirloom tomatoes

1 cucumber, peeled, halved lengthwise, seeded, and thinly sliced

4 radishes, shaved paper thin

¼ medium red onion, sliced paper thin

½ yellow bell pepper, cut into matchsticks

2 tablespoons red wine vinegar

¼ cup cilantro or tarragon leaves, chopped

¼ cup basil leaves, rolled and sliced into thin slivers

2 teaspoons hot sauce, such as Tabasco

4 large red leaf lettuce leaves

Up to 1 pound lump crabmeat, optional

The crabmeat is completely optional—it could just as easily be seared tuna, marinated tofu, or fresh mozzarella—and simply serves to make the salad a great lunch entrée. If opting for crab, pick over it and remove any shell fragments but do remember to handle it carefully to preserve the large, sweet chunks.

(recipe continues)

THE CUTTING BOARD CONUNDRUM

I can't tell you how often I encounter home cooks using nubbled glass cheese display boards as cutting boards. What a perfect way to ruin the most important tools in your kitchen, your knives. Same goes for marble, slate, concrete, sandpaper, or anything else hard and abrasive. Cutting boards must be made of a softer material, like wood or plastic. My main board is a wood one from Kūkhāven, a Michigan company created by my friends Charlie and Gretchen Spreitzer; it's thick and heavy and doesn't move around. I use plastic boards for meats. Some people use a special color (often red) for meats, which helps avoid cross-contamination; for me, once I've used a board for meat, it goes straight into soapy water.

1 Preheat a grill, grill pan, or broiler to high.

2 Brush both sides of the bread with olive oil and grill until golden brown, about 2 minutes per side. Cut 1 of the garlic cloves in half and rub one side of each toast with the garlic. Sprinkle the toasts with salt, cut into 1-inch squares, and set aside.

3 Slice the tomatoes into bite-size chunks and place them in a large bowl, taking care to catch any juices on the cutting board and direct them into a small bowl. Add the cucumber, radishes, onion, and bell pepper to the tomatoes.

4 To make the vinaigrette, chop the remaining 2 garlic cloves, then add 1½ teaspoons salt, and mash into a paste with a sturdy fork. Add to the small bowl with the reserved tomato juices along with the vinegar, cilantro, basil, and hot sauce. Then, whisking constantly, add the olive oil in a thin stream to combine.

5 To assemble, place 1 leaf of red leaf lettuce on each of 4 plates. Add the croutons to the tomato mixture, drizzle with vinaigrette, and toss gently so as not to break up the tomatoes. Taste for seasoning, add salt if needed, and divide the mixture in unruly piles on the plates. Put the crabmeat in the empty tomato bowl and toss very gently to absorb the remaining dressing. Divide among the plates, give thanks that February is far, far away, and serve.

Winter Salad OF WATERCRESS, FENNEL, AND ASIAN PEAR

SERVES 4 GENEROUSLY OR 6 AS A SIDE SALAD

I'VE ALWAYS THOUGHT grocery stores should display posters telling you which fruits and vegetables are in season and at their best. Of course, supermarkets would never do that, because they want people in Wisconsin to buy tomatoes and cantaloupes even when it's February. Instead, make a salad with foods that *are* good in winter: these. A lively Asian vinaigrette with lemongrass and a hint of nutty sesame is perfect against the sweet, crunchy pear.

1 small fennel bulb, tops removed

1 small Asian pear

2 bunches of watercress, tough stems removed (4 generous cups)

1 large or 2 small shallots, thinly sliced

1 tablespoon minced peeled fresh ginger

1 tablespoon minced tender lemongrass stalk

2 tablespoons fresh lime juice

1 tablespoon rice vinegar

1 tablespoon extra-virgin olive oil

½ teaspoon toasted sesame oil

½ teaspoon kosher salt

A grind or two of fresh black pepper

1 Thinly slice the fennel and Asian pear using a mandoline or sharp knife. Put in a large bowl along with the watercress and shallot.

2 In a small bowl, whisk together the ginger, lemongrass, lime juice, rice vinegar, olive oil, sesame oil, salt, and pepper. Pour over the salad, and toss to combine.

Asian pears look like tan apples and share the crunch of an apple but have a lovely, floral sweetness that is unmistakably pear flavor. They are juicy and refreshing and play nicely in salads with bright vinaigrettes.

MÂCHE AND HERB Power Salad SERVES 4

A LOT OF PEOPLE think of herbs mainly as flavorings to add to their cooking, but here they play a starring role. Not only does this simple salad pack a powerful wallop of bright, fresh, green flavor, its vivid aromas are fantastic on the table. Meanwhile, mâche (pronounced "mosh") is a truly great, incredibly tender green, and is now available in most better grocery stores. If you can't find it in yours, just use baby romaine, mesclun, or another flavorful green for your base, because that's what those greens are here: the backup singers.

4 cups mâche or mixed baby greens

½ cup flat-leaf parsley leaves

½ cup basil leaves

¼ cup strong fresh herbs, such as chives, chervil, tarragon, or dill

2 tablespoons red wine vinegar

¼ cup extra-virgin olive oil

Kosher salt and freshly ground black pepper

¼ cup slivered almonds or pine nuts, toasted

1 In a large bowl, combine the greens, parsley, basil, and other herbs. Put the vinegar in a small bowl, and, whisking constantly, slowly drizzle in the olive oil in a thin stream. Season the vinaigrette with salt and pepper.

2 Dress the salad with the vinaigrette, tossing to coat the leaves. Sprinkle the nuts on top, and serve.

Many professional chefs like to garnish a meat, fish, or pasta dish with tiny versions of herb salads like this one—a great touch. If you're using this *that* way, go for a higher proportion of the strong herbs, or even use *only* herbs.

Haricots Verts and Baby Greens WITH
FINGERLINGS AND PESTO VINAIGRETTE SERVES 4

AS MUCH AS I like pesto, incorporating it into a vinaigrette laid bare a shortcoming: it lacks acidity. A little tang from white wine vinegar makes it even yummier. It also makes an excellent dressing for French green beans and creamy, golden fingerling potatoes, which just seem to need to be together.

You could bang out the pesto in a food processor, but grinding it the old-school way into a paste (hence "pesto," of course) in a mortar and pestle is fast and fun; it also seems to inform your dish with a history, a soulfulness from everything you ever mashed in that battered, fragrant bowl. I use a Mexican molcajete, carved from volcanic stone.

PESTO VINAIGRETTE

- 1 tablespoon pine nuts, toasted
- 1 teaspoon coarsely chopped garlic
- 1 teaspoon coarsely chopped shallot
- ½ cup packed basil leaves
- 1 tablespoon freshly grated Parmesan cheese
- 1½ tablespoons Champagne or other white wine vinegar
- ⅓ cup extra-virgin olive oil
- Kosher salt and freshly ground black pepper

SALAD

- ½ small red onion, sliced paper thin
- 4 (½-inch) slices baguette
- Extra-virgin olive oil, for brushing
- 1 garlic clove, peeled and sliced in half
- Kosher salt
- ½ pound fingerling potatoes, cut into ½-inch pieces
- ½ pound haricots verts, cut into 2-inch lengths
- 2 good handfuls of baby greens

1. Make the pesto: Combine the pine nuts, garlic, and shallot in a mortar and grind into a paste. Add the basil leaves, and grind them into the mix. Stir in the Parmesan, vinegar, and olive oil, and season with salt and pepper, and set aside.

2. Make the salad: In a small bowl, soak the onion in ice water to reduce the sharpness.

3. Heat a grill pan or skillet over medium-high heat. Brush the baguette slices with olive oil and toast on both sides until golden brown, 1 to 2 minutes per side. Rub each on one side with the garlic clove, sprinkle with salt, and cut into 1-inch croutons.

4. In a large bowl, prepare an ice bath, and place a colander in the sink. In a medium saucepan filled halfway with water, bring the water to a boil and season well with salt. Add the potatoes and cook for 6 minutes. Add the beans to the potatoes, and continue cooking until both the beans and potatoes are tender but not too soft, 3 to 4 minutes. Drain in the colander, then plunge the colander into the ice bath to stop the cooking.

5. To serve, toss the greens with some of the vinaigrette, then divide among 4 plates. Toss the beans and potatoes with vinaigrette, and divide over the greens. Drain the onion, pat dry with paper towels, and sprinkle over the salads along with the croutons. Serve at once.

HOW TO MAKE DELICIOUS HOMEMADE WINE VINEGAR

Maybe this has happened to you: You have friends over for dinner. It's an occasion, so you open some nice wine. At the end of the evening, you stuff corks in the unfinished bottles. But several days later you still haven't polished them off, the stuff is undrinkable, and you find yourself dumping an expensive delicacy down the drain. And this makes you sad.

HERE'S A BETTER IDEA:

With just a little effort, you can turn those leftover wines into the most delicious vinegars you've ever tasted.

On kitchen counters in wine-loving countries like France, it's common to find an earthenware crock with a spigot for just this purpose. Good cooks know that vinegar is one of the most important ingredients in the pantry, that essential acidic element in so many dishes, and the crucial component in vinaigrettes. Even the cheapest wine you drink is almost certainly higher quality than the stuff used by most commercial vinegar companies, meaning your vinegar will be better and more complex (and, basically, free). You don't even need special equipment. All you need is a large jar, a paper towel, a rubber band, and a couple of months. Well, that's almost all you need.

FIRST, SOME EXPLANATION:

When wine is exposed to oxygen, it eventually turns to vinegar all by itself. You could just let your leftovers sit around in bottles, but you can speed and improve the process dramatically with more oxygen and a little "mother of vinegar," the harmless bacteria that converts alcohol into acetic acid. You've probably seen a mother in older bottles of unpasteurized vinegar; it's the slimy gunk that forms at the bottom. (You won't find it in most commercial vinegars; they're pasteurized to kill the bacteria because it looks unappetizing.) You can get raw vinegar containing a mother from any health-food store, online, or from home-brewing or winemaking shops; a tablespoon or two is plenty.

ANY KIND OF WINE WILL WORK—RED, WHITE, CHAMPAGNE, DESSERT.
Or for that matter, almost any kind of quality ale or hard cider—as long as it contains alcohol. Pour the liquid into clean jars, add some mother, cover with a paper towel (this allows oxygen in and keeps fruit flies out), snap on the rubber band, and leave the jar in a dark place. In a couple of weeks, you should see a skin forming on the top; that's the new mother. You don't want to disturb this skin, or it will sink to the bottom and stop doing its job, and you'll lose time while another skin forms.

AFTER TWO MONTHS, START TASTING.
Carefully nudge a straw around the edge of the mother and into the liquid, put your finger over the other end of the straw, and draw off enough to taste. (Here's where it would be an advantage to have a spigot in the jar, so you could draw vinegar from the bottom without disturbing the mother.) If it still tastes wine-y and doesn't have enough tang, give it a couple more weeks and taste again. If it's too tart, add water. When the vinegar tastes good to you, strain it and bottle it; recycled wine bottles are great for this, as are those beer bottles with the white porcelain-and-rubber stoppers. It'll taste better than any vinegar you can buy, and it makes a great gift.

Summer Sweet Corn WITH JALAPEÑO AND HERB BUTTER SERVES 4

LIKE TOMATOES, SWEET CORN is one of those summer-only treats made all the more special by its ephemera. You can grill it, nuke it, steam or boil it, as you like—they all work well. I prefer the grill. And while presenting corn on the cob is certainly beautiful and fun, I like to do the work for my friends and shave off the kernels; this also makes it much easier to get other flavors into the mix. Plus, the serving of corn you get from a single cob is not enough, in my view. For four people, I want six to eight cobs.

8 ears of corn

¼ cup extra-virgin olive oil

2 tablespoons unsalted butter, softened

1 garlic clove, minced

1 teaspoon kosher salt

½ jalapeño chile, or more to taste, seeded and chopped

1 Preheat a grill or grill pan to high.

2 Pull the husks back on the ears of corn, but keep them attached. Remove the silks with a firm scrub brush under running water. Pat the corn dry with kitchen towels, and brush it with the olive oil. Replace the husks, place the ears on the grill, and cook, turning onto all sides, until the kernels are tender and husks are blackened, 10 to 12 minutes.

3 While the corn cooks, in a small bowl, mix together the butter, garlic, salt, and jalapeño.

4 Use a sharp knife or "corn zipper" to remove the corn kernels, reserving any sweet liquid that collects on the cutting board, and transfer them to a large bowl. Toss the kernels and any reserved juices with the jalapeño butter, taste for heat and seasoning, and keep warm until ready to serve.

You can, of course, serve this on the cob, with the husks on, which makes for a beautiful presentation (and keeps the corn warm longer). Put the butter in small ramekins and serve alongside.

Pink Grapefruit and Avocado Salad

THE TECHNIQUE OF simmering liquids such as wine and stock to concentrate their flavors is a simple and crucial one, and you see it in many dishes. But I only recently came across the idea of reducing citrus juice for a salad dressing. Herewith, how to make grapefruit taste more like grapefruit, a lovely foil to the creamy avocado and crispy Boston lettuce.

2 to 3 large pink grapefruits, as needed

2 ripe Hass avocados, halved, pitted, peeled, and cut into ½-inch pieces

1 large or 2 small heads of Boston lettuce, leaves torn into bite-size pieces

1 teaspoon Dijon mustard

1 tablespoon sherry vinegar

3 tablespoons extra-virgin olive oil

1 teaspoon kosher salt

½ teaspoon freshly ground black pepper

1 tablespoon chopped chives

1 Slice off the tops and bottoms of 2 of the grapefruits, removing the peel and pith and just the tiniest bit of flesh. Work your way around each fruit, doing the same, so that you are left with 2 peeled, pith-free grapefruits. Over a glass measuring cup, slide a paring knife between the grapefruit membranes to release the citrus segments; put them in a large bowl. Squeeze the membranes in the cup to get out every bit of juice. You need 1 cup juice; if you don't have a cup of juice, squeeze enough of the additional grapefruit to produce the right amount.

2 Pour the grapefruit juice into a saucepan and bring to a boil over medium-high heat. Reduce the heat and simmer until there is about ¼ cup left; this will take 15 to 20 minutes. Transfer to a small bowl to cool.

3 Add the avocado and lettuce to the grapefruit segments.

4 In a small bowl, whisk together the mustard, vinegar, and reduced grapefruit juice. In a slow stream add the olive oil, whisking all the time, until the dressing is emulsified. Mix in the salt, pepper, and chives and toss gently with the grapefruit, avocado, and lettuce. Serve right away.

However-Many-Bean and Crunchy-Veg Salad WITH MUSTARDY VINAIGRETTE SERVES 8 TO 10 AS A SIDE DISH

I MAKE THIS salad all summer long, a little differently each time, depending on what's ripe. It's easy-breezy, fresh, colorful, and crispy. And it's a great example of the kind of room-temperature dish that to me defines summer picnic life; almost everything on the table is served room temp (except meats) and family style, with a scoop and a smile. Here, I've opted for two kinds of beans; it's just as good with one. Or three.

2 garlic cloves

Kosher salt and freshly ground black pepper

¼ cup red wine or cider vinegar

1 tablespoon Dijon mustard

¾ cup extra-virgin olive oil

2 cups 1-inch-sliced yellow wax beans

1 (15-ounce) can black beans, rinsed and drained

3 celery ribs with leaves, coarsely chopped

3 medium carrots, coarsely chopped

1 yellow bell pepper, cored, seeded, and coarsely chopped

½ medium red onion or 1 big shallot, chopped

1 tomato, coarsely chopped

1 jalapeño chile, seeded and finely chopped

Kernels cut from 2 ears of sweet, in-season corn

1 To make the vinaigrette, chop the garlic, add ½ teaspoon salt, and then mash into a paste with a fork. Scrape into a medium bowl and add the vinegar and mustard. Whisking constantly, add the olive oil in a thin stream until emulsified.

2 In a medium saucepan, heat an inch of water to boiling, add 1 tablespoon salt, and add the wax beans. Cook for 2 to 4 minutes, or to your desired doneness, tasting after 2 minutes to check. Remove with a slotted spoon and plunge into cold water to stop the cooking. Drain well.

3 In a large bowl, toss the wax and black beans, celery, carrots, bell pepper, onion, tomato, jalapeño, and corn with the dressing. Season to taste with salt and pepper. Serve immediately or chill, if desired; this salad is great either way.

When it's hot out and I want to keep effort to a bare minimum, I don't emulsify the dressing first. I just dump the vinaigrette ingredients on top of the salad and toss—and it turns out fine.

CRISPY NUTTY BLACK-EYED PEA SALAD FOR A CROWD SERVES 20

These proportions yield enough for a pretty good-sized group; make it a day ahead and refrigerate if you'd like.

Make a double recipe of the mustardy vinaigrette, opposite, and stir in ⅓ cup chopped tarragon leaves. Cut 1 (12-ounce) package duck bacon (such as that sold by D'Artagnan) into ½-inch dice. In a Dutch oven over medium-low heat, fry the bacon until crispy, about 8 minutes, remove with a slotted spoon, and reserve. Add 1 chopped medium red onion to the bacon fat along with 2 chopped celery ribs, and cook until softened, about 7 minutes. Add 1½ pounds dried black-eyed peas, water or chicken stock to cover by an inch, and 1 teaspoon kosher salt. Bring to a boil, reduce the heat, and simmer until just tender, 20 to 30 minutes, checking occasionally to make sure the peas are barely covered by water. Do not overcook; better for the peas to be slightly crunchy than mushy. When the peas are al dente, drain and cool. Add the bacon and about three-quarters of the dressing, adding more to taste. Season with salt and freshly ground black pepper, and serve.

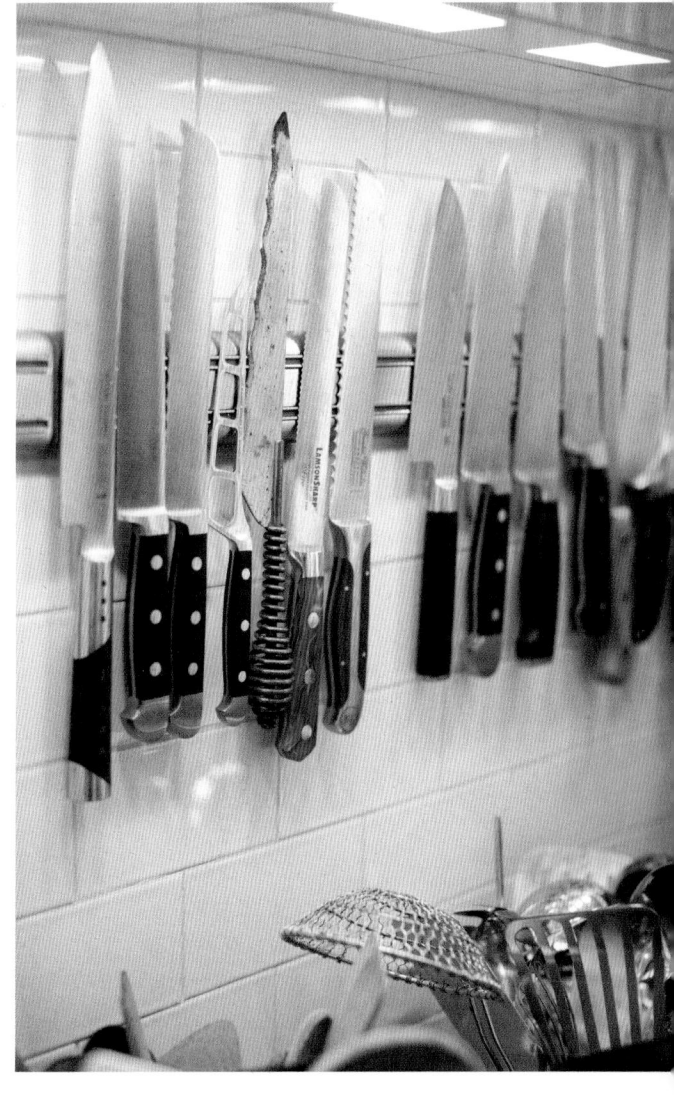

Wiggly Rice Noodle and Herb Salad

THE CONCEPT OF cooking Italian pasta until it's just al dente—"to the tooth"—is widely known. Here, a rapid-cooking technique is also used to preserve the texture of those very thin Asian rice noodles labeled "rice stick." You drop a pouf of these translucent noodles into hot water, steep them for a few minutes, and they quickly puff up and turn a pretty white. But rice noodles behave differently than wheat; there's a jolliness to them, a bouncy, springy wiggliness, both in the way they move when you handle them and in the way they chew. For me, it's that perfect chewiness that defines this noodle's character. Also, rice stick is a wonderful sponge for flavor, instantly absorbing the tangy, nutty, earthy flavors of this dressing.

1 cup snow peas

2 medium carrots, peeled and thinly sliced on the diagonal

2 scallions (white and green parts)

4 ounces thin rice-stick noodles

1 pound medium shrimp, peeled and deveined

1 teaspoon sugar

2 tablespoons plus 2 teaspoons fresh lime juice

1 tablespoon plus 1 teaspoon fish sauce

1½ teaspoons toasted sesame oil

½ cup plus 1 tablespoon chopped cilantro leaves

½ cup chopped mint leaves

2 tablespoons low-sodium soy sauce

2 tablespoons hoisin sauce

1 teaspoon Sriracha sauce, or more to taste

1 teaspoon honey

2 tablespoons vegetable oil

1 Fill a large saucepan with salted water, and bring to a boil. Prepare an ice bath in a large bowl. Add the snow peas to the boiling water, cook for 1 minute, and remove with a slotted spoon to the ice bath to cool. Repeat with the carrots. Thinly slice the peas, and cut the carrots into similarly sized matchsticks. Cut the scallions into 1½-inch sections and then thinly slice lengthwise into matchsticks.

(recipe continues)

2 Keep the pan of water on the stove but turn off the heat underneath it. Add the noodles and let steep in the hot water for 5 minutes, then drain well, and put in a large bowl.

3 Meanwhile, in a bowl, mix together the shrimp, sugar, 2 teaspoons of the lime juice, 1 teaspoon of the fish sauce, $1/2$ teaspoon of the sesame oil, and 1 tablespoon of the cilantro.

4 Add the snow peas, carrots, scallion, mint, and remaining $1/2$ cup cilantro to the rice noodles.

5 In a small bowl, mix the soy sauce, hoisin sauce, remaining 2 tablespoons lime juice, remaining 1 tablespoon fish sauce, remaining 1 teaspoon sesame oil, the Sriracha, and honey. Pour over the noodles and toss to combine.

6 Heat a large skillet over medium-high heat until hot, about 5 minutes. Swirl the vegetable oil around the pan (it will smoke a little until you add the shrimp) and quickly add the shrimp and any marinade. Cook the shrimp until pink and just cooked through, about 2 minutes per side. Add the noodles and stir to mix in the shrimp, or let the shrimp cool, mix into the noodles, and serve the dish at room temperature.

SPICY Cucumber and Pineapple Salad

SERVES 6 TO 8 AS A SIDE DISH

CUCUMBER AND PINEAPPLE—you wouldn't think, would you? This salad is always a hit with our crowd. It leans Asian, so it's a nice accompaniment to many foods from that corner of the world. I particularly like it for a cookout, where its sweet-and-sour nature works well with the sweetness and smoke of grilled, sauced meats. It's great with my barbecued ribs (page 195).

⅔ cup unseasoned rice vinegar (or, in a pinch, white vinegar)

⅔ cup sugar

½ teaspoon table salt

Grated zest of 1 lemon

1½ cups bite-size chunks of fresh pineapple

1 hothouse cucumber, peeled, halved lengthwise, seeded with a small spoon, and sliced ¼ inch thick

½ yellow bell pepper, cut into matchsticks

2 shallots, sliced paper-thin

½ to 1 jalapeño chile, to taste, seeded and finely diced

¼ cup cilantro leaves

1 tablespoon sesame seeds, toasted

1 Heat the vinegar, ½ cup water, the sugar, and salt in a saucepan over high heat until the sugar and salt dissolve. Cool the mixture to room temperature and then stir in the lemon zest.

2 Combine the pineapple, cucumber, bell pepper, shallots, jalapeño, and cilantro in a plastic storage container with a lid and pour the dressing over. Add the sesame seeds and toss to coat. Marinate, refrigerated, for at least 1 hour for the flavors to blend, or up to 4. Serve cold or at room temperature with a slotted spoon.

GRILLED Green Beans WITH HARISSA   SERVES 4

MOST FOODS ARE improved by an introduction to charcoal and smoke, and that includes those that hang from beanstalks. The only trick is not losing half of your green beans to the fire, a job made easier with one of those mesh cages for grilling smaller foods. Me, I just do my best to keep them perpendicular to the grates, and I have my average casualties down to about three beans. A quick toss in a vinaigrette spiked with spicy North African chile paste, aka harissa, really livens things up; in a pinch, you could use the same amount of Sriracha, or just Tabasco with a chopped garlic clove. Or, if you prefer, skip the heat—these are still really good.

Kosher salt

1 pound green beans, trimmed

2 teaspoons vegetable oil

1 tablespoon red wine vinegar

1 tablespoon extra-virgin olive oil

1 teaspoon harissa

1 Preheat a grill or large grill pan to high.

2 Prepare a large bowl of ice water; set aside. Fill a large saucepan halfway with water and bring to a boil over high heat. Season the water generously with salt. Add the beans and blanch until just crisp-tender, 2 to 4 minutes. Drain, and plunge the beans into the ice water for 2 minutes to stop the cooking. Drain the beans and pat dry with kitchen towels.

3 Put the beans in a large bowl and toss with the vegetable oil. Using tongs, arrange in a single layer on the grill and cook until lightly charred, 3 to 5 minutes.

4 Whisk together the vinegar, olive oil, harissa, and 1/2 teaspoon salt in a large bowl. Add the warm beans, toss, and serve warm or at room temperature.

ROASTED **Sunchokes** WITH MUSHROOMS AND ROSEMARY

SERVES 6 AS A SIDE DISH

SUNCHOKES, ALSO CALLED Jerusalem artichokes, are neither artichokes nor Israeli. And, as they are actually the root of a plant, it's hard to argue that they have much relationship to the sun. They are, however, a tuber from a species related to sunflowers, which starts to explain *one* of those names. More important than any of this: they are absolutely delicious, something like a cross between a potato, an artichoke, a water chestnut, and a turnip, but better. They're a little starchy when raw, but slightly sweet and nutty when roasted. Great for a puree. Here, they dovetail beautifully with earthy mushrooms and piney rosemary.

1 pound sunchokes

3 tablespoons extra-virgin olive oil

1 teaspoon kosher salt

½ pound mushrooms, such as cremini, cut in 1-inch chunks

1 tablespoon chopped rosemary leaves

1 tablespoon unsalted butter

1 Select a 2-quart (or so) oven-safe gratin dish with a lid; then place the dish—but not the lid—in the oven, and preheat it to 450°F.

2 Scrub but do not peel the sunchokes, and cut into 1-inch chunks. Immediately toss with the olive oil to prevent discoloration. Season with ½ teaspoon of the salt.

3 Wearing oven mitts, remove the dish from the oven, carefully add the sunchokes (reserving the bowl and leftover olive oil), which will sizzle excitingly, and 2 tablespoons hot tap water. Cover, and return to the oven. Bake for 10 minutes.

4 While the sunchokes cook, toss the mushrooms in the oil remaining in the bowl, and season with the remaining ½ teaspoon salt. Wearing oven mitts, remove the hot dish once again from the oven, and add the mushrooms, rosemary, and butter. Stir to combine, leave the dish uncovered, and roast the veggies until tender and easily pierced with the tip of a knife, 10 minutes.

HONEY-GLAZED Baby Root Vegetables WITH GREENS

SERVES 4 TO 6

I WAS WAITING in line at our farmers' market when the farmhand asked the woman in front of me, "Want me to cut the tops off those beets?" I almost leaped into one of those slow-motion movie moments to stop him: "Nooooo!" It's bad enough that supermarkets whack off the tops of beets, celery, turnips, radishes—all edible, all delicious—and waste them. But an organic farmer at a local market? He should be passing out recipe ideas for those greens! I consoled myself with the fantasy that the farmhand had such a strong addiction to beet tops that he hoarded them in bushels for himself. Then, the next week, I gave him this recipe.

1 pound baby golden beets or turnips, greens attached

1 pound radishes, greens attached

3 garlic cloves, peeled

¼ cup extra-virgin olive oil

2 teaspoons thyme leaves, plus some whole sprigs for garnish

2 teaspoons honey

1 teaspoon kosher salt

1 tablespoon unsalted butter

1. Wash the beets and radishes, and peel the beets (wear rubber gloves if you don't want to stain your hands). Cut radishes in half lengthwise, taking care to leave some greens attached to each root piece, and cut beets lengthwise until they are the same size as the radishes. Put the veggies in a sauté pan with a lid, add the garlic and olive oil, and toss to coat. Add ¾ cup water, the thyme leaves, honey, and salt, and bring to a boil over high heat. Cover the skillet, reduce heat to medium-low, and simmer, shaking the skillet occasionally, until the vegetables are tender and pierced easily with the tip of a knife, 12 to 15 minutes.

2. Transfer the vegetables to a serving platter, draping the soft greens around the roots in pleasing swirls. Bring the cooking liquid back to a boil, remove from the heat, and swirl in the butter. Pour the sauce over the vegetables, garnish with sprigs of thyme, and serve.

The secret here is in finding small, baby veggies, or carefully cutting them all to the same small size lengthwise without cutting off the stems. Shoot for about half the size of a golf ball. If you detach a few greens, it doesn't matter. Cook 'em anyway!

Roasted Beet and Asparagus Salad
WITH QUADRELLO AND GARLIC VINAIGRETTE SERVES 4

THIS BEAUTIFUL SALAD uses the beet greens as well as the root. (If you can't find beets with greens on, you can use Swiss chard.) Soft, slightly funky Quadrello cheese, made from raw buffalo milk, pairs beautifully with the earthy sweetness of the beets, though you could certainly substitute Taleggio or another soft, washed-rind cheese.

4 medium beets with greens attached, well scrubbed

2 garlic cloves, unpeeled, cut in half

5 tablespoons extra-virgin olive oil, plus more for drizzling

Fine sea salt and freshly ground black pepper

16 medium asparagus spears

Pinch of sugar

3½ teaspoons red wine vinegar

2 ounces Quadrello cheese, cut into 4 pieces

1 Preheat the oven to 400°F.

2 Cut the greens from the beets. Remove and discard the stems, and tear the leaves into bite-size pieces. Set aside.

3 Put the beets and garlic on a piece of foil in a small roasting pan. Drizzle with some olive oil, and sprinkle with salt and pepper. Bring the foil up around the beets to cover, and roast until tender, 50 minutes to 1 hour.

4 While the beets roast, heat an ovenproof sauté pan over medium-high heat for 5 minutes. Add 1 tablespoon of the olive oil and then the asparagus, and season with salt and pepper. Transfer the pan to the oven and roast until the asparagus are browned and lightly cooked through, about 6 minutes. Remove and set aside.

5 When the beets are done, remove from the oven and slip off the skins while still warm. Cut into bite-size pieces.

6 Squeeze the roasted garlic out of its skins onto a cutting board. Sprinkle with a generous pinch of salt, a couple grinds of black pepper, and the sugar, and mash into a paste with a fork. Put the garlic paste in a small bowl, add the vinegar, and then whisk in 3 tablespoons of the olive oil in a thin stream until emulsified. Taste, adding more salt and pepper if needed.

7 In a sauté pan set over medium-high heat, warm the remaining 1 tablespoon olive oil. Leaving some moisture on the greens after washing, toss them into the pan, season with a little salt and pepper, and cook, stirring occasionally, until tender, about 4 minutes.

8 Arrange 4 asparagus spears on each of 4 plates. Toss the greens with half of the vinaigrette, and then place atop the asparagus. Gently toss the beets in the remaining vinaigrette, and divide among the plates on top of the greens. Add a piece of cheese to each plate, and serve.

CLEARING THE AIR

This is about a built-in feature of your kitchen, so unless you're renovating, you're probably going to file this in the back of your mind for the next house. But if you *are* planning a new kitchen, I strongly recommend that you make this a top priority: a really good vent hood with a powerful fan—and make sure it's the kind that blows exhaust outside, not a recirculating model. (Unfortunately for us New Yorkers, in many apartment buildings, this is impossible; c'est la vie.) If possible, get an in-line fan with a motor that can be installed outside, rather than in the hood itself—it's an enormously lovely thing to exhaust smoke and heat without it sounding like a plane is landing on your countertop.

Herewith, also, an argument for buying a range instead of a cooktop and a wall oven: with a range, your hood can ventilate heat from your oven as well as the stove, a real plus when you're, say, roasting a turkey or baking in July.

Why is ventilation so important? Because so much good cooking happens at high temperatures and produces spatter, aerosolized grease, and, of course, smoke. There are foods that you simply cannot cook without proper ventilation—for example, there is no way to properly panfry a steak without getting your pan red-hot and making great, gushing clouds of beefy smoke. With a true, powerful hood, you can do this without occasioning a visit from the fire department; do it without one, and they'll be pounding on your door with axes in hand, plus you'll need to clean your carpets, furniture, and your entire wardrobe. Extra bonus: using the hood whenever you sauté keeps your kitchen much cleaner. The hood in our kitchen sucks up aerosolized grease that would otherwise have settled on our cabinets and countertops, and traps most of it in stainless-steel, dishwasher-safe filters.

Heirloom Beans WITH PORK, SOFFRITTO, AND SMOKE SERVES 10 TO 12 AS A SIDE DISH

I USUALLY COOK beans with soffritto and a smoked ham hock, flavors that beautifully complement their creamy sweetness (see page 82). The goal: most of the beans should retain their shape and be tender but not mushy; however, some of them should break up and impart creaminess to their liquid, known in the South as pot likker. For more thickness, stick an immersion blender into your finished beans and puree a little, or just do some smooshing with a potato masher or spoon. I like black beans, pintos, red beans, cannellini, black-eyed peas, and flageolets. Sometimes I add spices such as cumin or cayenne; other times not. Sometimes, a cup of diced tomatoes. Not today.

1 pound dried beans

2 tablespoons extra-virgin olive oil

1 medium yellow onion, chopped

1 celery rib, chopped

1 medium carrot, chopped

2 garlic cloves, chopped

1 bay leaf

2 teaspoons chili or chile powder, optional

1 teaspoon ground cumin, optional

¼ teaspoon cayenne or 1 chopped seeded jalapeño chile

1 smoked ham hock (preferably) or 3 slices smoked bacon or ham, diced

3 sprigs fresh thyme, tied together with cotton string

Kosher salt and freshly ground black pepper

1 to 2 tablespoons red wine vinegar, to taste

Serve these on their own, as a bed for roasted meat or poultry, or (best of all) over cooked brown or white rice.

(recipe continues)

IT'S ALL ABOUT THE SOFFRITTO

Unless you're Puerto Rican, rather than Italian, in which case it's all about the *sofrito*. If you're French, as it happens, it's all about the mirepoix. For us Americans, what all of this is all about is the holy aromatic trinity of onions, carrots, and celery, gently sizzling in a shimmer of olive oil. You'll find soffritto all over the place in this book. It's the base for most of my soups, bean dishes, braises, and tomato sauces for pasta; it's as important in chicken stock as the chicken is. It is the backbone of flavor development for so, so many dishes in so many cultures. The perfume of soffritto is such a promise of great tastes to come. Time-saver: one day, when you're bored, make a gigantic batch of it, divide it into one-pint containers, and freeze it; you'll have at least a half-hour jump start on a million different dishes down the road.

1   Rinse and pick over the beans, discarding any small stones or other debris. If you have time, put the beans in a bowl, cover with water by 2 or 3 inches, and soak for up to 6 hours. If not, just plan on simmering them a little longer.

2   In a large Dutch oven or stockpot over medium heat, warm the oil, and then cook the onion, celery, and carrot until tender, about 8 minutes. Add the garlic, bay leaf, and, if using, chili powder, cumin, and/or cayenne, and cook until fragrant, about 1 minute. Add the beans, ham hock, thyme, and water to cover the beans by about 1 inch. Bring to a boil, reduce the heat, and simmer gently, partially covered, for 30 minutes. Add 1 teaspoon salt and simmer for 30 minutes.

3   After an hour, spoon out a few beans and taste for tenderness. Keep cooking and testing as needed, checking at least every 15 minutes, as things speed up toward the end of the process. Add small amounts of hot water, if needed. When the beans are tender and the liquid is creamy and thickened, they're ready. Remove the bay leaf. If you want thicker liquid, hit the mixture briefly with the immersion blender. Season with salt and pepper as needed before serving.

For an easy bean soup, just add more water or stock at the end of the process, being sure to adjust the seasoning with salt and pepper; you can serve as is, or puree the soup and pass it through a strainer (see opposite) for a more refined result.

THE "CHINA CAP" STRAINER

If you make your own stocks or pureed soups—and why wouldn't you?—please tune in. One of my favorite tools in the kitchen, and one that goes completely unheralded, is also one of the most labor-saving and food-improving you'll ever buy: the China cap, aka the chinois (online, most spell it incorrectly with a final "e"), or, in English, the fine-mesh strainer. I'm talking about pro-grade, conical strainers with handles, of which I have two—one coarse, with ⅛-inch holes, one dual-layered superfine mesh, both reinforced so I can force thick liquids through them while leaving solids behind. Get yourself this duo and suddenly it's so much easier to strain chicken stock (no more messy cheesecloth, or failing to *have* cheesecloth) or to strain pureed soups of root vegetables or beans. And your resulting products will be more refined.

NUT-ROASTED Brussels and Broccoli SERVES 6 TO 8

IT SEEMS ALMOST every time I'm describing something delicious, from toast to cheese to beer, I'm using the word "nutty." In this simple dish, two vegetables that already take on pronounced nutty qualities when roasted come together with (what else?) nuts, both for flavor and a bit of crunch. Blanching and shocking are extra steps—you could, of course, just roast the vegetables and call it a day—but don't. Blanching locks in vivid green color that will otherwise fade in the oven.

⅓ cup almonds

Kosher salt

1 pound Brussels sprouts, trimmed and halved

1 pound broccoli florets, trimmed to the size of a Brussels sprout

2 tablespoons extra-virgin olive oil

Grated zest of 1 lemon

1 Preheat oven to 450°F.

2 Put the almonds in a food processor and pulse several times; you want a mix of large chunks for crunch and finely ground nuts that will cling to the vegetables.

3 In a large pot, bring 2 inches of water to a boil and season generously with salt. In a large bowl, prepare an ice bath. Add the Brussels sprouts to the boiling water, bring back to a boil, and cook for 2 minutes. Then add the broccoli and cook for 2 minutes. Quickly drain in a strainer, and then plunge the strainer into the ice bath to chill for 2 minutes. Drain well.

4 Heat a large, cast-iron or other ovenproof skillet over medium-high for 5 minutes. Add the olive oil and then the vegetables, nudging the sprouts cut side down to encourage browning. Toss in the almonds. Transfer the skillet to the oven. Roast until the vegetables are tender and golden brown with a little bit of char on the edges, 5 to 7 minutes.

5 Add ½ teaspoon salt, and toss to combine. Sprinkle with the lemon zest, and serve in the skillet.

PROVENÇAL Vegetable Gratin

THIS IS A peak-of-summer southern French classic, and a great way to showcase tomatoes and zucchini when they're abundant. Besides height-of-season produce, the key to the success of this dish is draining some of the vegetable juices so the gratin isn't watery.

1 pound zucchini, sliced crosswise into ¼-inch rounds

1 pound yellow squash, sliced crosswise into ¼-inch rounds

2 teaspoons fine sea salt

1½ pounds medium heirloom tomatoes, preferably a mix of red and yellow, sliced into ¼-inch slices

1 tablespoon unsalted butter

4 tablespoons extra-virgin olive oil

2 medium yellow onions, halved and thinly sliced

1 tablespoon thyme leaves, chopped

2 garlic cloves, minced

1 cup dried coarse bread crumbs

1 cup freshly grated Parmesan cheese

To make this vegan, leave out the Parmesan and grease the dish with olive oil.

1 Put the zucchini and squash in a large bowl, and sprinkle with 1 teaspoon of the salt, tossing a couple of times as you sprinkle, so all pieces get seasoned. Dump onto a large cooling rack over kitchen towels (or straight onto the towels), and let drain 45 minutes. Press the top with additional towels to dry the surface.

2 Meanwhile, arrange the tomato slices in one layer on kitchen towels and sprinkle with ½ teaspoon of the salt; let sit for 30 minutes. With additional towels, lightly press on the tomatoes to remove more juice.

3 Preheat the oven to 400°F. Grease a 9 × 13-inch baking pan or large gratin dish with the butter.

4 In a large sauté pan, heat 1 tablespoon of the oil over low heat, add the onion and remaining ½ teaspoon salt, and cook until soft and golden, 25 minutes.

5 In the gratin dish, layer the zucchini and squash, sprinkling with half of the thyme, half of the garlic, and 1½ tablespoons of the olive oil. Spread the onions evenly over the squash, and then layer the tomatoes, overlapping slightly, to cover. Sprinkle with the remaining garlic, thyme, and 1½ tablespoons olive oil. Bake, uncovered, for 35 minutes.

6 In a medium bowl, blend the bread crumbs and Parmesan. Remove the pan from the oven, and increase the oven temperature to 450°F. Sprinkle the veggies with the Parmesan topping. Return the gratin to the oven and bake until the top is browned, up to 10 minutes, and serve.

Roasted Radicchio WITH BALSAMIC AND GARLIC

SERVES 4 AS A SIDE DISH

BITTER ITALIAN CHICORY tossed in sweet vinegar and roasted it 'til it's burned? Sign me up! I think foods with a certain controlled bitter quality are wonderful, and radicchio responds really well to the oven (and the grill, too). The inner leaves get tender, while the outer ones begin to burn at the edges, creating a delicate crispiness. Meanwhile, balsamic vinegars (especially aged ones) are every bit as much about sweetness as they are about tang, and that property intensifies in the heat of the oven, balancing the dish. Bonus points: this dish is gorgeous—I want to wallpaper my dining room with the photo spread on the previous pages—costs pennies, is perfect to prep ahead, and couldn't be easier.

1 large round head radicchio

4 teaspoons plus 2 tablespoons extra-virgin olive oil

1 garlic clove

¼ teaspoon kosher salt

⅛ teaspoon freshly ground black pepper

⅛ teaspoon sugar

2 teaspoons balsamic vinegar

2 teaspoons thyme leaves

1 Preheat the oven to 450°F.

2 Remove the outer leaves from the radicchio. From the top, cut into quarters. In a large bowl, toss the radicchio wedges in 4 teaspoons of the olive oil to coat. Transfer to a baking sheet, cut sides up.

3 Chop the garlic on a cutting board. Sprinkle with the salt, pepper, and sugar, and, using a fork, mash into a paste. Scoop the garlic paste into a small bowl and mix in the balsamic. Whisking continuously, add the remaining 2 tablespoons oil in a thin drizzle, and then add the thyme. Spoon evenly over the radicchio.

4 Roast the radicchio until tender on the inside and browned—even slightly charred—on the outside, 12 to 15 minutes. Serve quickly.

PERFECT-EVERY-TIME **Baked Rice** SERVES 4

CHEF AARÓN SANCHEZ, one of my beloved *Chopped* compadres, comes from a culture that knows a little about rice. So when he told me on set that his restaurants have always baked theirs, rather than prepping it on the stovetop or in rice cookers, my ears perked up. The advantages are many, among them, the pot never boils over, the tendency to peek midway is reduced, and rice never burns on the bottom of the pan. In the main, though, it's just simpler to let your oven keep things at a precise temperature than it is to do so yourself up top.

Whenever you're using a pan in the oven, don't forget the oven mitts, please. And after taking a hot pan out of the oven, *immediately* slip a mitt over the handle.

1 tablespoon extra-virgin olive oil or unsalted butter

1 teaspoon kosher salt

1½ cups long-grain white rice or short- or medium-grain brown rice

1 Preheat the oven to 375°F.

2 In a medium ovenproof saucepan with a tight-fitting lid, bring 2½ cups water to a boil and add the oil and salt. Stir in the rice, cover, and transfer to the oven. Bake until the rice is tender and has absorbed all the water, about 18 minutes for white rice or 1 hour for brown. Let rest a moment, stir, and serve.

This recipe works with white or brown rice. I particularly like basmati—it smells like popcorn!

For more flavor and aroma:
- Substitute homemade chicken stock (page 173) for water
- Add ½ teaspoon crushed saffron
- Add ½ teaspoon ground cumin
- Add 5 cardamom pods
- Add 1 teaspoon chopped rosemary or thyme leaves before baking, or 1 teaspoon chopped dill, parsley, or cilantro leaves after

Duck Fat Potatoes WITH PARSLEY AND LEMON SERVES 4 TO 6

THE FRENCH HAVE KNOWN this forever, whereas here, in the beautiful States, it just became the next big thing: there is nothing more wonderful you can do to potatoes than to cook them in duck fat. Where do I get duck fat, you ask? Cook a single Moulard duck breast half, and you'll easily render off a cup and a half (see page 140). Strain out the brown bits, and you can store the fat almost indefinitely in the fridge. And don't feel guilty—you're using only a tiny bit.

1½ pounds fingerling potatoes, sliced in half lengthwise

3 tablespoons duck fat, melted

1 teaspoon kosher salt

½ teaspoon freshly ground black pepper

¼ cup chopped flat-leaf parsley leaves

1 teaspoon grated lemon zest

1 tablespoon fresh lemon juice

1 Preheat the oven to 450°F.

2 In a mixing bowl, toss the fingerlings, duck fat, salt, and pepper to coat. Spread in an even layer on a baking sheet and roast until the cut sides of the potatoes are golden and crispy, 25 to 30 minutes.

3 Transfer to a serving bowl, and mix in the parsley, lemon zest, and juice. Serve hot.

Macaroni and Cheese WITH AGED GOUDA AND CHEDDAR SERVES 4 TO 6

IN THIS GROWN-UP version of nature's perfect food, the Cheddar is the backbone, unctuous and sharp, while the salty-crunchy aged Gouda plays beautifully with its noble Italian cousin, Parmesan. Brown it well and crisp it up. Lots of cheese and just a bit of cream; that's the way I like it.

Kosher salt and freshly ground black pepper

1 pound dried macaroni elbows, ziti, or penne

1¼ to 1½ cups fresh bread crumbs

¼ cup flat-leaf parsley leaves, chopped

1 medium garlic clove, minced

2 tablespoons extra-virgin olive oil

3 tablespoons unsalted butter

¼ cup all-purpose flour

3 cups whole milk

1 cup heavy cream

⅛ teaspoon freshly grated nutmeg

1 bay leaf

8 ounces aged Gouda, finely grated (about 2 cups)

6 ounces Cheddar cheese, finely grated (about 1½ cups)

¼ cup freshly grated Parmesan cheese

1 Preheat the oven to 400°F.

2 Bring a large pot of salted water to a boil, add the pasta, and cook until almost cooked through, 7 to 11 minutes, depending on the pasta. You want the noodles just underdone, because they will be seeing more heat.

3 Meanwhile, put the bread crumbs in a bowl and stir in the parsley, garlic, and oil.

4 Drain the pasta very well in a colander and set aside. Heat the pot over low heat, add the butter, and let it melt. Add the flour and stir for 1 minute until the mixture bubbles. Turn the heat to medium. Gradually add the milk in a fine stream, whisking all the time, and then the cream; the sauce will thicken as it comes to a simmer.

A good rule of thumb when cooking pasta: 2½ teaspoons kosher salt per quart of water or, as my chef pal Alex Guarnaschelli says, until it tastes like the ocean. Salted water takes longer to boil, so season *after* your water is heated.

Aged Gouda is a very different cheese from the soft, mellow stuff wrapped in red wax. It's harder, crumbly, and much more flavorful; it's orange and filled with little salty enzyme crystals similar in texture to Parmigiano-Reggiano that give it a little crunch when you bite into it. It's one of my favorites.

A six-inch piece of baguette or a couple of slices of white bread, given a whirl in the food processor, should do the trick for the fresh bread crumbs. Don't bother to remove the crust.

Then add the nutmeg and bay leaf, and simmer, stirring constantly, particularly at the edges of the pot to keep the flour from burning, for 10 minutes to cook out the flour taste. Remove the bay leaf.

5 Add the cheeses and stir to melt them. Season with ½ teaspoon salt and ¼ teaspoon pepper. Add the pasta and mix well to combine. Spoon into a buttered 9 × 13-inch or 2-quart gratin dish and sprinkle with the bread crumb mixture. Bake until warmed through, bubbly, and lightly browned on the top, 20 to 25 minutes.

SILKY **Celery Root Puree** WITH WHISKEY ONIONS SERVES 6

PUREES OF ROOT VEGETABLES are such a lovely foundation for meat, poultry, and fish dishes—there's nothing like having something lush, soft, and rich alongside crispy chicken skin or the charred crust of a steak. All due respect to potatoes, there are several vegetables that do purees even better, notably celery root (aka celeriac). It's a homely veggie until it's cooked and whipped up, at which point it boasts a glossy silkiness that potatoes never get without a ton of cream. Top these off with whiskey onions—caramelized onions finished with a little sweet, smoky bourbon—and you're gonna get some rave reviews.

3 tablespoons extra-virgin olive oil

2 medium white or yellow onions, thinly sliced (2 cups), plus 1 small white or yellow onion, cut into 1-inch chunks

¼ cup bourbon

Kosher salt and freshly ground black pepper

3 cups whole milk

1 teaspoon thyme leaves or 1 bay leaf

2½ pounds celery root (about 2 large), peeled and cut into 1-inch chunks

1 medium russet potato, peeled and cut into 1-inch chunks

3 tablespoons unsalted butter, softened

1 In a sauté pan over medium heat, warm the olive oil, and add the sliced onions. Cook, stirring often, until caramelized and deeply golden-brown, but not burned, about 25 minutes. Add the bourbon, and cook, stirring, for 1 minute. Season with salt and pepper, and remove from the heat.

2 In a large saucepan, bring to a boil the milk and 3 cups water. Add 1 tablespoon salt, the thyme or bay leaf, and the celery root, potato, and onion chunks. Bring to a boil, reduce the heat to medium, and simmer until the vegetables are tender, about 30 minutes. Drain, reserving a cup of the cooking liquid in case the puree needs to be thinned (though it probably won't need to be). Discard the bay leaf if using.

3 Combine the celery root mixture with the butter in a food processor and puree. The mixture should be soft and silky, but able to hold a soft peak. Taste, season with salt and pepper, and spoon into a warm serving dish. Top with the caramelized onions, and serve.

Main Courses

Asian Beef Tenderloin FOR A CROWD SERVES 8

MY FRIEND LIZ HOLLAND is famous for her roasted beef tenderloin and (ahem) hollandaise—it's her go-to when she's feeding a crowd. Here, I take a similarly French approach to steak au poivre, meaning encrusted in black pepper, and give it an Asian spin with Szechuan peppercorns. A long marinate in soy, sesame, garlic, and ginger brings deep, warm flavor.

½ cup low-sodium soy sauce

2 tablespoons mirin

2 teaspoons toasted sesame oil

2 tablespoons packed light brown sugar

8 large garlic cloves, minced

3 tablespoons minced peeled fresh ginger

8 scallions (white and green parts), chopped

1 medium yellow onion, grated

1 medium Asian pear, grated

1 (4½-pound) beef tenderloin roast, tied

3 tablespoons coarsely ground Szechuan peppercorns

2 tablespoons extra-virgin olive oil

1 In a large bowl or baking dish, combine the soy, mirin, sesame oil, brown sugar, garlic, ginger, scallions, onion, and Asian pear, and stir to combine. Add the beef and turn to coat. Cover and marinate in the refrigerator for at least 4 hours, preferably overnight.

2 Preheat the oven to 500°F.

3 Put the ground Szechuan peppercorns on a plate. Remove the beef from the marinade, scraping off all the solids, and roll it in the peppercorns, pressing down so that they stick.

4 Heat a large, ovenproof skillet over medium-high heat for 5 minutes, then add the olive oil. Put the beef in the pan and sear on all sides until well browned, about 10 minutes. Then, transfer the roast to the oven and bake until an instant-read thermometer inserted into the thickest part of the roast reads 130°F, about 15 minutes.

5 Remove from the oven and tent with foil for 15 minutes for perfect medium-rare, 20 minutes for medium. Slice and serve.

Szechuan peppercorns are not, actually, peppercorns; in fact, they are the outer pod of a tiny fruit, used widely as a spice throughout Asia. They have a vaguely lemony overtone and produce a faint tingling sensation on the palate. You can find them in Asian markets.

Belgian Beef Stew WITH BEER, ONIONS, AND HERB SPAETZLE SERVES 6 TO 8

IF YOU'VE NEVER cooked the Belgian classic Carbonnade à la Flamande, you'll be amazed at its spicy heartiness, made sweet with ale and onions, and its unique assembly. Find yourself a frosty Sunday afternoon, and dive in.

4 strips of bacon, diced

3 pounds beef stew meat, trimmed of excess fat and cut in 2-inch cubes

Kosher salt and freshly ground black pepper

1½ pounds yellow onions, halved and sliced ¼-inch thick (6 cups)

2 garlic cloves, minced

1 teaspoon thyme leaves

1 bay leaf

1 teaspoon cayenne

¼ teaspoon allspice (optional)

2 tablespoons Dijon mustard

2 slices crusty whole-grain, sourdough, or pumpernickel bread

2 cups Belgian-style golden ale, lambic, or Abbey ale

2 cups beef stock, preferably homemade (page 173), or low-sodium store-bought

1 tablespoon packed light brown sugar

1 tablespoon red wine vinegar

Herb Spaetzle (optional; recipe follows)

1   Preheat the oven to 325°F.

2   In a Dutch oven, brown the bacon over medium heat, about 8 minutes, and transfer with a slotted spoon to a plate lined with a paper towel. Reserve the bacon fat in the pot.

I usually opt for golden ale rather than a heavy, Abbey style, and prefer more stock in ratio to beer than you'll find in most traditional recipes. Sometimes, I veer even further from the classic by tossing in carrots and turnips for the last hour of cooking. This is typically served over boiled potatoes, but is also excellent with noodles, rice, or—especially—spaetzle (recipe follows).

(recipe continues)

A word on browning the meat for this stew: do not try to do it all at once, or you will overcrowd the pan and the meat will boil in its juices rather than properly brown. A good sear is a key to developing great flavor.

3 Spread the beef evenly on a cutting board or baking sheet and season well all over with salt and pepper. Raise the heat under the pot to high and brown the beef on all sides in two batches, at least 10 minutes per batch, using a spatter screen if you have one. Remove the meat to a bowl.

4 Reduce heat to medium, add the onions, season with a little salt, and cook, scraping up the brown bits from the pot, until golden brown and soft, 10 minutes. Add the garlic, thyme, bay leaf, cayenne, and allspice (if using), and cook, stirring, until fragrant, 1 or 2 minutes. Transfer the onion mixture to a bowl.

5 Spread the mustard on each side of the 2 slices of bread. Put half the beef and all of the bacon back into the pot. Put the bread slices on the meat, and then smother with half of the onions. Add the remaining meat and then the remaining onions. Mix the ale and stock with the brown sugar and vinegar, and pour into the pot, completely covering the stew ingredients. Over high heat, bring the stew to a strong simmer, then transfer to a low rack in the oven, and braise until the beef is tender, 2 to 2½ hours. Discard the bay leaf before serving.

Herb Spaetzle SERVES 6 TO 8

ONE OF MY FAVORITE noodles in the world, and it's not Italian or Asian? You got it. This homey German classic takes to herbs somehow more beautifully than any other noodle; its irregular blob shapes catch sauce gorgeously, and give a delightfully meaty chew. You can plop the dough into the water in small spoonfuls, or press it through the holes of a colander or box grater (my favorite way to go). Frying the noodles is optional—but what makes them truly great.

2 cups all-purpose flour

1 teaspoon fine sea salt, plus more for the water

1 teaspoon baking powder

4 large eggs

2/3 cup whole milk

1/4 cup minced fresh chives

3 tablespoons unsalted butter

1 teaspoon freshly ground black pepper

If you have a potato ricer with large (3/16- to 1/4-inch) holes, use it to make the spaetzle.

1 In a medium bowl, stir together the flour, salt, and baking powder. In a small bowl, beat the eggs and milk, and stir in the chives. Add to the flour mixture, and stir until the flour is evenly moistened and you have a sticky dough. Cover with plastic wrap and set aside to rest briefly.

2 Put a large pot of water over high heat, bring to a rapid boil, and generously salt—about 2 tablespoons per quart of water. Set a colander with large, 1/4-inch holes on top of the pot, and, using the back of a large, sturdy spoon, press the dough through the holes and into the boiling water. Cook until the spaetzle float to the top, about 3 minutes. Remove with a slotted spoon to a second colander to drain.

3 Put a large nonstick or cast-iron skillet over medium-high heat, and add the butter. When the butter has melted and begins to sizzle, add the spaetzle and cook for 2 to 3 minutes without stirring to form a golden crust. With a spatula, flip to the other side and cook for 2 minutes. Remove from the heat, season with the pepper, and tuck right in.

Grilled Skirt Steak WITH ROASTED JALAPEÑO CHIMICHURRI SERVES 4

PEOPLE WHO haven't worked a lot with jalapeños, Scotch bonnets, anchos, guajillos, and poblanos might not realize that these different spicy chiles also have pronounced and unique flavors—or that those flavors change when the peppers are roasted or grilled. Here, the grassy-herbal jalapeño picks up a bittersweet char on the grill and still lends its familiar kick to this variation on garlicky South American chimichurri sauce. And there's no better cut for this recipe than juicy, chewy-in-the-best-way skirt steak, grilled just to medium-rare.

2 jalapeño chiles

2 cups finely chopped cilantro leaves and sprigs

2 cups finely chopped parsley leaves and sprigs

2 garlic cloves, minced

3 tablespoons fresh lime juice

3 tablespoons dry red wine

1 tablespoon red wine vinegar

½ cup extra-virgin olive oil, plus more for brushing

Kosher salt and freshly ground black pepper

2 pounds skirt steak

1 Preheat a grill or grill pan to high.

2 Roast the jalapeños on the grill until charred on all sides. Put in a bag or covered bowl to steam and cool a little; then peel, stem, and seed the chiles.

3 Put the jalapeños, cilantro, parsley, garlic, lime juice, red wine, vinegar, olive oil, and salt and pepper to taste in a blender and pulse to blend. Taste for salt, adding more if needed, and blend again.

4 Brush the steak with olive oil and generously season both sides with salt and pepper. Grill the steak, turning once, until medium rare, 2 to 4 minutes per side, depending on thickness. Transfer to a plate, tent with foil, and let rest 5 to 10 minutes. Slice the steak ½ inch thick across the grain with the knife blade tilted at a 45-degree angle, pile on a serving platter, and top with some chimichurri; pass extra sauce at the table.

ULTIMATE Spaghetti and Meatbrawls
WITH SERIOUS SUNDAY GRAVY   SERVES 6 TO 8

THERE IS ALMOST nothing I would rather cook than this. But what kind of adventure or discovery could possibly lurk in an über-traditional spaghetti and meatballs? Plenty, unless your Nonna has already taught you the secrets of slow-cooked Sunday Gravy. This is an authentic sugo (Italian for sauce), really not a tomato sauce at all, but something far more special. In fact, a single can of tomatoes is at most a supporting actor.

Instead, this sugo is all about the soffritto—that is, gently sautéed aromatic vegetables—and an enormous amount of stock (which, if you think about it, is also largely about soffritto) made intensely flavorful by simmering until it's reduced fully by half. The sauce comes out not red, but a vivid orange with an olive-oily sheen. It is a thing of depth and beauty. Yes, it takes some time and labor to make, as do these soft, spicy meatbrawls (I just like calling them that), with their traditional combination of beef and pork. But they're both so delicious, now and then you just have to devote the time.

MEATBALLS

1 pound ground beef

½ pound ground pork

½ medium yellow onion, finely chopped

2 garlic cloves, finely chopped

¼ cup flat-leaf parsley leaves, chopped

½ cup freshly grated Parmesan cheese

⅓ cup fresh bread crumbs (made from stale bread)

⅓ cup chicken stock, preferably homemade (page 173), or low-sodium store-bought

2 large eggs

½ teaspoon cayenne

1½ teaspoons kosher salt

3 tablespoons extra-virgin olive oil, plus more for forming meatballs

GRAVY

2 tablespoons extra-virgin olive oil

2 medium yellow onions, chopped

2 celery ribs, chopped

1 large carrot, chopped

3 garlic cloves, chopped

2 bay leaves

1 tablespoon tomato paste

1 (28-ounce) can chopped San Marzano tomatoes

3 quarts chicken stock, preferably homemade (page 173), or low-sodium store-bought

2 or 3 sprigs of fresh thyme, tied together with cotton string

½ cup basil leaves, chopped

Skip the meatballs and use veggie stock, and you have an unbeatable vegan entrée.

(recipe continues)

Sometimes I speed the plow by buzzing up the onions, garlic, celery, parsley, and carrots in a food processor, but if you have time, the texture of hand-chopped is better.

I am a big fan of the Italian kind of tomato paste that comes in the resealable tube, which means I don't waste an entire can when I need only a tablespoon.

You can skip the step of frying the meatballs if you like, but it adds a lot of flavor and helps them hold their shape. So, in fact, no, you can't.

I like thick spaghetti for the sauce, but penne, farfalle (bowties), or linguine are fine, too. Pass freshly grated Parmesan at the table for sprinkling on top.

1 Make the meatballs: In a large bowl, using your hands, mix together the beef, pork, onion, garlic, parsley, Parmesan, bread crumbs, stock, eggs, cayenne, and salt until evenly combined. Be careful not to overwork the mixture; you don't want to compact the meat too much or the meatballs will be tough. Put a little oil on your hands and form loosely into golf-ball-size meatballs. You should have about 25.

2 Heat the olive oil in a large Dutch oven over medium heat. Gently add the meatballs and brown thoroughly on all sides; this will take about 15 minutes. Transfer the meatballs to a plate, and refrigerate until you're ready to cook them in the sugo.

3 Make the gravy: In the same pan you used to cook the meatballs, heat the olive oil over medium heat and add the onions, celery, and carrot. Cook, stirring occasionally, until soft, about 8 minutes. Add the garlic and bay leaves and cook until fragrant, 1 minute. Push the veggies to one side and add the tomato paste, toasting it on the bottom of the pan for 1 minute. Stir into the vegetables.

4 Add the tomatoes, chicken stock, and thyme, and bring to a boil. Reduce the heat and simmer very gently, partially covered, until thick and significantly reduced, about an hour.

5 Carefully add the meatballs, a few at a time, and simmer, stirring very gently now and then—don't break-a ya bawls!—until cooked through, 40 minutes. Discard the bay leaves and thyme sprigs. Add most of the basil and stir, reserving a little to sprinkle over the top for serving.

Herbed Roast Chicken WITH CHARRED POBLANO SAUCE SERVES 4

RUBBING HERB BUTTER under the skin of the breast produces an obscenely moist and flavorful roast whole chicken. Here, I use cilantro and oregano, but rosemary, thyme, sage, tarragon, or a blend thereof would also be great. Try this under-the-skin technique with pesto, too—delicious. Meanwhile, a simple sauce of roasted poblano chiles, jalapeño, and cider vinegar adds piquancy and pep. Most poblanos have little or no spiciness, hence the jalapeño. But I always add chiles gradually to a recipe, because no two chiles pack exactly the same heat. Some poblanos can surprise you!

2 tablespoons unsalted butter, at room temperature

1 tablespoon extra-virgin olive oil

2 tablespoons chopped cilantro leaves

1 tablespoon chopped fresh oregano or 1 teaspoon dried

1 tablespoon chopped garlic

1 lemon, zested and quartered

½ teaspoon kosher salt

¼ teaspoon freshly ground black pepper

1 (4-pound) chicken

Charred Poblano Sauce (recipe follows)

1 Preheat the oven to 400°F.

2 In a small bowl, mix the butter with the olive oil, cilantro, oregano, garlic, lemon zest, salt, and pepper.

3 Using your index finger, and working from the back end of the bird, carefully separate the skin from the breast meat. Now, here's a trick: Unless your fingers are 9 inches long, you won't be able to separate the skin and breast all the way to the front of the chicken. To do this, I use the handle of a table knife that's slightly fat and rounded on the edges, so as to not tear the skin. This way I can separate the skin all the way to the neck.

4 Then, using a small spoon, stuff about one-third of the herb butter under each breast half, massage it throughout the pocket, then rub the rest over the outside of the bird. Finally, stuff the lemon quarters into the chicken's cavity. Tie the legs together with cotton string, tuck the wingtips under the chicken's body, and put the chicken on a rack in a shallow roasting pan.

Double or triple the herb butter and freeze the extras in a small ramekin with plastic wrap on top; it's great to have around for bread, to stir into a sauce, or just to save time on the next roast chicken.

(recipe continues)

5 Roast in the oven until the skin is golden brown, the legs wiggle easily, and the breast meat reads 175°F on an instant-read thermometer, about 1 hour 15 minutes. Remove from the oven, tent with foil, and give the bird at least 15 minutes to rest so that the juices are reabsorbed throughout the meat. (Otherwise, the juices will end up on your cutting board, wasted.) Cut into 10 pieces (drumsticks, thighs, wings, and breast halves, with breasts chopped in half crosswise to produce 4 pieces) to serve with the warm poblano sauce on the side.

Charred Poblano Sauce MAKES ABOUT 2 CUPS

3 poblano chiles

1 jalapeño chile

½ large red onion, peeled and cut into four pieces

2 garlic cloves, peeled

½ cup chicken stock, preferably homemade (page 173), or low-sodium store-bought

1½ tablespoons cider vinegar

1 cup (loosely packed) flat-leaf parsley leaves

1½ teaspoons kosher salt

1 Using a grill, broiler, or a gas burner set on high, roast the poblanos and jalapeño on all sides until their skins are almost completely blackened and charred, about 10 minutes. Put in a bag or covered bowl and allow to steam and cool a little.

2 Wearing rubber gloves if necessary, rub off the skins, and discard the seeds and stems. Cut the jalapeño in half crosswise (you only need about half for this recipe but you have to roast the chile whole). Puree the poblanos, half jalapeño, onion, garlic, stock, vinegar, parsley, and salt in a food processor until smooth. Taste at least two bites for spiciness, giving your palate time for the heat to hit; if desired, puree in another slice or two from the reserved jalapeño half. In a small saucepan, warm the sauce gently over medium-low heat before serving.

Chicken Tacos
WITH CHIPOTLE SOUR CREAM SERVES 2

IT'S TACO TUESDAY! Or any day! Who wouldn't overuse exclamation points?! I loved taco night when I was a kid, when it meant yellow cheese, seasonings from a packet, and machine-molded tortilla shells—essentially, an insult to all of Mexico in one convenient box. It is, of course, better to make real tacos with sweet fresh flour tortillas.

1 tablespoon extra-virgin olive oil

1 medium red onion, chopped

½ red bell pepper, cored, seeded, and chopped

2 teaspoons smoked sweet paprika

2 teaspoons chili powder

1 teaspoon dried oregano

½ teaspoon ground cumin

½ teaspoon kosher salt

2 garlic cloves, minced

1 medium tomato, chopped

2 cups shredded cooked chicken

6 (6-inch) flour tortillas

2 teaspoons minced canned chipotle peppers in adobo

½ cup sour cream

Shredded lettuce

3 scallions (white and green parts), chopped

Crumbled queso fresco (fresh, white Mexican cheese)

1 In a sauté pan over medium heat, warm the oil and cook the onion, bell pepper, paprika, chili powder, oregano, cumin, and salt until the veggies are soft, 7 minutes. Add the garlic and cook until fragrant, 1 minute. Stir in the tomato and chicken, and cook until the filling is heated through, stirring, about 3 minutes.

2 Warm the tortillas in moistened paper towels in the microwave for 30 seconds, or for a few seconds in a dry skillet over high heat. Stir the chipotle into the sour cream.

3 Pile the filling into the tortillas, topping with chipotle sour cream, lettuce, scallions, and queso fresco.

Chicken Quesadillas
WITH BROCCOLI RABE SERVES 2 AS A SNACK

FOR ME, QUESADILLAS are the quintessential place to park leftover chicken. A few common pantry spices, sweet red onion to balance the bitter rabe, funky/earthy cumin to go up against grassy-hot chile—these all complement the raison d'être of a quesa-D: crispy tortilla meats gooey cheese. Especially good at 2 a.m.

Kosher salt

2 to 3 sprigs of broccoli rabe, cut in bite-size pieces

1 tablespoon extra-virgin olive oil

½ medium red onion, thinly sliced into rings

2 teaspoons chili powder

½ teaspoon ground cumin

1 garlic clove, finely chopped

2 teaspoons finely chopped jalapeño chile

2 (6-inch) flour tortillas

⅔ cup shredded Monterey Jack cheese

⅔ cup shredded cooked chicken

Salsa and sour cream, for serving

1 Fill a medium saucepan halfway with water, bring to a boil, and season with salt. Add the broccoli rabe, and blanch until the stems are crisp-tender, about 4 minutes. Drain, dry, and set aside.

2 Wipe the pan dry and add the olive oil; then, over medium heat, cook the onion, chili powder, cumin, and ½ teaspoon salt until the veggies are soft, about 7 minutes. Add the garlic and jalapeño, and cook until fragrant, about 1 minute.

3 Put 1 of the tortillas in a large, dry skillet. Spread the onion mixture evenly over the tortilla, and then sprinkle the cheese on top. Add the chicken and broccoli rabe; then top with the second tortilla.

4 Cook over medium heat, turning once, until the tortilla is crispy and the cheese is melted through, about 5 minutes per side. Cut into wedges, and serve with salsa and sour cream.

Risotto WITH CHICKEN AND PEAS SERVES 2

THIS DISH IS REASON enough to always have a little cooked chicken and some peas in the freezer—and, of course, some Parm in the fridge. Risotto is a staple these days, and great to have in one's cooking arsenal; it's comforting, it's cheap, and it's tops for filling up the troops in a hurry. Adding hot stock to the rice only when it's ready to absorb it allows the rice to give off its starch, adding body to the sauce.

5 to 6 cups chicken stock, preferably homemade (page 173), or low-sodium store-bought

½ medium yellow onion, chopped

2 tablespoons extra-virgin olive oil

1 cup Arborio rice

1 garlic clove, chopped

½ cup dry white wine

1 cup chopped cooked chicken

½ cup frozen peas

½ cup freshly grated Parmesan cheese

1 Heat the chicken stock to a simmer in a medium pan and keep hot.

2 In a larger pan on the very next burner—I like the two pans to touch so you're less likely to spill stock onto the stove—sauté the onion in the olive oil until soft, about 7 minutes. Add the rice and garlic, and sauté for 3 minutes. Add the wine and simmer, stirring, until the rice absorbs it, another 3 minutes.

3 Check your watch, and, stirring often, start adding the warmed broth with a ladle, half a cup at a time, letting the rice absorb each ladleful before adding another. Keep the rice at a gentle simmer. After 15 minutes, start tasting the rice to get a feel for its doneness—you want it cooked through, but not mushy; it should take about 18 minutes total. When the rice is almost there, add the chicken, peas, and Parmesan. Add stock as needed so the risotto is soft and soupy. Mound the risotto into the centers of 2 plates, and serve immediately. (Eat from the outside in so the middle stays hot!)

CHICKEN LEFTOVERS **Stew** SERVES 4

WHEN I CAME UP with this recipe, it was 25°F outside, the wind was howling, and there were two feet of leftover snow turning gray and crusty on the ground. In happier news, there was also leftover roasted chicken in the fridge, along with potatoes and turnips, and green beans in the freezer. How could I *not* make stew?

2 tablespoons extra-virgin olive oil

2 medium carrots, cut into ¼-inch-thick coins

1 medium yellow onion, chopped

2 celery ribs, chopped

1 medium garlic clove, chopped

2 teaspoons chopped jalapeño

2 tablespoons all-purpose flour

3 cups chicken stock, preferably homemade (page 173), or low-sodium store-bought

½ pound red potatoes, cut in 1-inch chunks

½ pound turnips, cut in 1-inch chunks

1 bay leaf or ½ teaspoon dried thyme

2 cups shredded cooked chicken

2 cups cut green beans

1 cup grape tomatoes, cut in half

½ cup flat-leaf parsley—or, if you prefer, cilantro—leaves

Salt and freshly ground black pepper

This is more of a guide than a recipe; adapt it based on how much chicken you have, what kind of vegetables are sitting around, and how salty your stock is. With a good mix of vegetation and a hunk of crusty bread, you've got yourself an easy, soulful, and deeply nutritious meal.

1 In a medium stockpot or Dutch oven over medium heat, warm the olive oil and sauté the carrots, onion, and celery until cooked through, about 8 minutes. Add the garlic and jalapeño and cook for 1 minute. Add the flour, and sauté, stirring frequently, for 3 minutes to cook out the floury taste.

2 Add the chicken stock, 1 cup water, the potatoes, turnips, and bay leaf, bring to a simmer, and cook until the vegetables are tender, about 15 minutes. Add the chicken, green beans, tomatoes, and parsley, and cook for a few minutes more. Discard the bay leaf, season with salt and pepper, and serve.

Chicken and Merguez Tagine WITH
CHICKPEAS, FENNEL, AND APRICOTS SERVES 6

THE WORD "TAGINE" is both the name of the clay pot synonymous with Moroccan cooking and the one-pot meal cooked inside of it. Use the pot once, and you'll understand why it has its distinctive, cone-shaped lid: you're adding ingredients and spice in layers so that each gets the right amount of cooking time—just as in a stir-fry, only with no stirring—piling them up in a heap that is tallest in the center (as heaps tend to be). The imperfect stir-fry analogy also fits regarding difficulty; this is an incredibly easy way to cook. The list of ingredients is long, but once they're chopped, it's just a matter of piling them into the tagine at the right time. As you cook, spices bloom and develop in the heat, vegetables give up their juices, meats and bones simmer and build a stock. Taste as you go—you'll really feel the dish coming to life.

1 teaspoon ground cumin

1 teaspoon ground coriander

1 teaspoon ground turmeric

½ teaspoon ground cinnamon

½ teaspoon fennel seed

¼ teaspoon cayenne

2 teaspoons kosher salt

1 (2½- to 3-pound) chicken, cut into 10 pieces (breast halves cut in half crosswise), skin removed

2 tablespoons extra-virgin olive oil

1 pound *merguez* (lamb sausage), cut in 2-inch pieces

¼ cup plus 1 tablespoon chopped cilantro leaves

1 large yellow onion, chopped

1 fennel bulb, tops removed, halved and thinly sliced

2 tablespoons chopped preserved lemon, homemade (recipe follows) or store-bought, or grated zest of 1 lemon

1½ tablespoons chopped, peeled fresh ginger

1 tablespoon chopped garlic

¼ cup chopped dried apricots

1 (15-ounce) can chickpeas, rinsed and drained

1 zucchini, quartered lengthwise and sliced crosswise ¼ inch thick

1 medium tomato, diced

½ orange bell pepper, cored, seeded, and diced

½ teaspoon harissa (optional), plus more for serving

2 tablespoons fresh lemon juice (optional)

Traditionally served with couscous, this is also delicious over rice or pearl couscous—which is actually pasta.

1 In a small bowl, mix together the cumin, coriander, turmeric, cinnamon, fennel seed, cayenne, and salt. Rub 2 teaspoons of the spice blend onto the chicken pieces.

2 Heat the olive oil in a tagine over medium-high heat for a few minutes, until just starting to smoke. Add the chicken and *merguez,* and brown on all sides, about 10 minutes.

You can cook a tagine in any stovetop-safe casserole or Dutch oven; it'll need to be at least 10 inches wide at the bottom and preferably have a domed lid. Or do what Barry did, and order a real, unglazed one like mine, below, at a reasonable price, direct from Morocco, at www.tagines.com. I don't recommend buying one from a fancy kitchen store; most are too small to hold even a tiny chicken, are glazed when they shouldn't be, and are seriously overpriced.

I prefer to remove the skin of the chicken because I find chicken skin cooked in liquid unappetizing, plus removing it makes the dish lighter; on the other hand, leaving it on provides more flavor. You pick.

3 Reduce the heat to low. Cover the chicken and sausage evenly with ¼ cup of the cilantro, the onion, fennel, preserved lemon, ginger, and garlic; sprinkle with 1 teaspoon of the spice blend, cover the tangine, and cook for 15 minutes.

4 Add the apricots, chickpeas, and zucchini, sprinkle with 1 teaspoon of the spice blend, cover, and cook for 15 minutes.

5 Add the diced tomato and bell pepper. Put a spoon in the broth and taste it. If it's well seasoned and spicy enough for you, stop adding spice; if you'd like more, mix the harissa into the lemon juice, and add it along with the last teaspoon spice blend. Cover and cook for 15 minutes.

6 Sprinkle with the remaining tablespoon cilantro, and serve, passing harissa at the table for people who want more heat.

PRESERVED LEMONS

Aside from harissa, *merguez,* and tagines, nothing says Moroccan cooking like preserved lemons. There's really no way to fake the mellowed flavor you get from lemons that have been cut, packed in salt, and pickled; lemon zest barely gets you halfway there. Fortunately, making preserved lemons is easy. These are great in everything from salads to cocktails, or for seasoning with an extra dimension besides salt. While you're at it, make a large batch of these and give a few jars to friends. Your reward will probably be at least one Moroccan feast!

For this purpose, buying organic lemons is important, because the peel is what you're going to be eventually eating; no pesticides, please.

Another thing: from November through March, when Meyer lemons are in season, consider preserving some of those, too; they have a different (and wonderful) flavor than regular lemons, being notably less tart.

MAKES 1 QUART

6 to 8 organic lemons, as needed
About 1 cup kosher salt
2 tablespoons extra-virgin olive oil

Wash the lemons thoroughly, then cut 6 of them lengthwise into quarters or eighths. In a clean, 1-quart mason jar, put 2 tablespoons salt, then toss each lemon wedge in salt and begin packing the wedges into the jar—and don't be shy, because the goal is for the lemons to give up their juices, which mix with the salt, and to be completely submerged in juice. Continue packing in salted lemon slices until you reach the top. If the lemons aren't completely covered in juice, cut another lemon, salt it, and cram those wedges in, too; if necessary, squeeze another remaining lemon and add the juice to the jar. When full almost to the lip, add olive oil to cover. Seal tightly with a lid. Let stand at room temperature for 2 to 5 days, gently shaking once a day. Store in the refrigerator for up to 6 months. When ready to use, rinse off salt, scrape away pulp, and use the peel (typically diced or julienned).

Thai Curry WITH CHICKEN AND FRESH NOODLES

SERVES 6 GENEROUSLY

OKAY, THIS ONE has a few moving parts; it will keep you busy for a while. But don't let that hold you back. It reads bigger than it is, and can be put together in an afternoon. We got this one from our friend Megan Schlow; the first time we tasted it at her Lower East Side apartment, Barry and I vacuumed it into our faces, splattering sauce onto our clothes, slurping every drop out of the bowl even while our eyes teared up and our mouths smoldered from the heat.

There is so much to discover here: First off, the fun of prowling an Asian market for lemongrass, tamarind, and shrimp paste. Second, the complexity—and flavor control—that comes from freshly made curry paste (take notes while you eat it so you can make adjustments next time and make it your own). Third, using southwestern/Mexican chiles in an Asian dish—they add flavor and body. Also, making a fresh stock and the universal wonder that is fried shallots. Be sure to hide them from your guests before you're ready to serve, or they *will* disappear long before the plates hit the table.

CHICKEN

2 pounds chicken breast on the bone

1 medium yellow onion, peeled and quartered

5 sprigs of cilantro

3 (¼-inch-thick) slices of ginger, each about the size of a quarter

1 Thai bird chile

Top of 1 lemongrass stalk

1 teaspoon kosher salt

CURRY PASTE

6 guajillo chiles, stemmed, seeded, and torn into a few pieces

2 árbol chiles, stemmed, seeded, and torn into a few pieces

2 tablespoons chopped peeled ginger

¼ cup chopped tender lemongrass stalk

¼ cup chopped cilantro leaves

3 small shallots, chopped

6 large garlic cloves, chopped

1 teaspoon shrimp paste

1 teaspoon curry powder

1 teaspoon turmeric powder

½ teaspoon kosher salt

STEW

2 tablespoons palm sugar or light brown sugar

2 tablespoons tamarind concentrate

2 tablespoons soy sauce

2 tablespoons fish sauce

2 (14-ounce) cans coconut milk

8 ounces fresh Chinese noodles, such as lo mein

½ cup crispy chow mein noodles

2 limes, cut into wedges

2 tablespoons fresh cilantro leaves

½ cup Fried Shallots (recipe follows)

1 cup Pickled Mustard Greens (recipe follows)

(recipe continues)

1 Cook the chicken: Put the chicken, onion, cilantro, ginger, chile, lemongrass, salt, and 12 cups cold water in a large pot over high heat. Bring to a boil, reduce the heat to low, and simmer until the chicken is just cooked through, about 30 minutes. Remove the chicken from the liquid and set it aside to cool, reserving the pot of liquid.

2 When the chicken is cool enough to handle, remove and discard the skin, shred the chicken into bite-size pieces, and set aside; return the bones to the stockpot. Simmer for 30 minutes. Turn off the heat and set aside to cool a little. Strain through a coarse China cap strainer (see page 83), then a fine one (or several layers of cheesecloth), discarding the solids and skimming off the fat from the top. Reserve 6 cups stock for the stew; freeze any extra.

3 Meanwhile, make the curry paste: Put the guajillos and árbols in a bowl, cover with hot tap water, and soak for 15 minutes. Gently lift the chiles from their soaking water and put in a blender along with the ginger, lemongrass, cilantro, shallots, garlic, shrimp paste, curry, turmeric, salt, and ½ cup water. Pulse the blender a few times to get things moving and then blend on high to form a smooth paste. Scrape into a bowl and set aside.

4. Cook the stew: Put a large pot over medium heat. Add the 6 cups chicken broth, palm sugar, tamarind concentrate, soy, and fish sauce and bring to a slow boil.

5. Reduce the heat, add the coconut milk and curry paste, and simmer for 30 minutes to combine all the flavors.

6. Meanwhile, cook the fresh noodles in a pot of boiling salted water until al dente, then drain, and keep warm.

7. Add the chicken to the stew and remove the pot from the heat. Put some cooked noodles into each bowl and top with the stew. Serve with crispy noodles, limes, cilantro, fried shallots, and pickled mustard greens for garnishing at the table.

Fried Shallots MAKES ABOUT 2 CUPS

½ cup vegetable oil

6 to 8 shallots, thinly sliced and separated into rings

½ teaspoon cornstarch

½ teaspoon table salt

1. Put a large skillet over medium-high heat and add the oil. Toss the shallot rings with the cornstarch to coat lightly. When the oil is hot but not smoking, add the shallots and fry until golden, 2 to 3 minutes.

2. Drain on paper towels and sprinkle with salt while hot. Hide from guests.

Pickled Mustard Greens MAKES 1 QUART

¼ cup rice vinegar

1 tablespoon table salt

1 teaspoon sugar

2 Thai bird chiles, split lengthwise

½ pound Chinese mustard greens, stemmed, cut into 1-inch pieces

1. In a saucepan over medium heat, combine 2 cups water, the vinegar, salt, and sugar, and bring to a boil. Remove from the heat, and add the chiles.

2. Pack the chopped mustard greens into a 1-quart jar and pour in the brine. When the greens are cool, they are ready. Cover and refrigerate for up to a week. Drain the greens before eating.

Chicken Paillards WITH PANCETTA AND SAGE SERVES 4

HERE'S MY SIMPLE, chicken-y take on saltimbocca. With just a paper-thin piece of pancetta, or a similar cured meat such as prosciutto, you can easily transform a chicken breast. The sage is both a flavorful and decorative touch.

4 boneless, skinless chicken breast halves

Kosher salt and freshly ground black pepper

1 large egg, beaten

12 sage leaves (8 whole, 4 chopped)

6 thin slices of pancetta

2 tablespoons extra-virgin olive oil

1 tablespoon unsalted butter

1 shallot, minced

1 tablespoon all-purpose flour

½ teaspoon thyme leaves

¼ cup dry white wine

1 cup chicken stock, preferably homemade (page 173), or low-sodium store-bought

1 Pound the chicken breasts to an even thickness of ¼ inch. Sprinkle with salt and pepper, and flip. Brush lightly with the egg. Press 2 sage leaves onto each piece of egged chicken, then cover with pancetta (about 1½ slices per breast), and press again. Refrigerate for 15 minutes.

2 Heat a large sauté pan over medium-high heat for about 5 minutes. When the pan is hot, add the olive oil and the chicken, pancetta side down. Cook until golden brown, about 3 minutes. Flip the chicken, and cook until cooked through, 2 to 3 minutes. Transfer to a warm plate and cover with foil.

3 Add the butter to the pan, reduce the heat to medium, and cook the shallot until soft, 3 minutes. Add the flour, stir, and cook for another 2 minutes. Add the thyme and wine, and deglaze, scraping up the brown bits; simmer for 3 minutes. Add the stock and chopped sage, and simmer until thickened, a few minutes. Serve the chicken on a pool of the sauce.

Grilled Chicken Breasts

WITH HARISSA SERVES 4

HARISSA, THE FIERY North African chile paste, is available in specialty food stores and some supermarkets. But if you don't feel like hunting for it just this minute, substitute Tabasco and one minced clove of garlic; the heat level is similar, and the main ingredients (chiles, vinegar, and salt) are similar enough. These breasts are great for a cookout, on their own, or on a bun.

6 tablespoons extra-virgin olive oil

2 tablespoons cider vinegar

1 tablespoon harissa

½ teaspoon kosher salt

4 boneless, skinless chicken breast halves

1 In a small bowl, whisk together the oil, vinegar, harissa, and salt. Put the chicken breasts in a zipper bag on a plate, add half of the harissa marinade (reserve the other half for basting), and refrigerate for at least 1 hour and up to 2 hours.

2 Preheat a grill or grill pan to medium-high.

3 Discard the marinade and pat dry the breasts. Grill for 5 minutes, turn, carefully baste with the reserved sauce, and grill until the chicken is cooked through, 4 to 5 minutes. Give a final gloss of sauce, let the chicken rest for a few minutes, and serve.

The larger lesson in these three techniques is that you can use other things for barding (say, American bacon), any kind of vinaigrette (balsamic would be nice), and all sorts of breadings—tempura batter, whole-wheat bread crumbs and sheep's cheese, sourdough bread crumbs and paprika— whatever you like.

Baked Chicken Breasts
WITH PARMESAN CRUST SERVES 4

NOW *HERE'S A* tasty piece of "oven-fried" chicken. A hint of mustardy tang, a little thyme, and a coating of toasty, Parmesan-y goodness all mean your house is going to smell great when you make this. Slice and fan the chicken across a bed of dressed greens, serve over rice, or put it on a roll for tailgating—it's good hot or cold.

2 tablespoons Dijon mustard

½ teaspoon thyme leaves, chopped

½ teaspoon kosher salt

¼ teaspoon cayenne

4 boneless, skinless chicken breast halves

¾ cup freshly grated Parmesan cheese

¾ cup Panko or dried coarse baguette bread crumbs

Cooking spray

1 Preheat the oven to 450°F.

2 Mix the mustard, thyme, salt, and cayenne in a medium bowl; add the chicken breasts; and turn to coat completely. Set aside.

3 In a medium shallow bowl, combine the Parmesan and bread crumbs. Dredge the chicken pieces in the crumbs, coating evenly and heavily, and pressing the coating into the meat.

4 Put the chicken on a rack set over a baking sheet, spray with a quick burst of cooking spray, and put the sheet in the middle of the oven. Bake until the chicken is golden and cooked through, 15 to 20 minutes. Let rest for 5 minutes before cutting or serving.

CRISP-TENDER Roast Duck WITH CHERRY-ROSEMARY SAUCE SERVES 4

NOW'S YOUR CHANCE to join me in the venerable Slow Food movement: This is an incredibly easy way to make a succulent roast duck with delicious cracker-crispy skin every time. The roasting technique comes from Sally Schneider's *A New Way to Cook,* which calls for making dozens of knife pricks in the skin, all over the bird, so that its huge stores of fat render out almost completely during a five-hour treatment in a low oven. The sauce is a perfect complement (great with pork, too) and is easy to make.

1 (5-pound) Pekin (aka Long Island) duck

Kosher salt and freshly ground black pepper

1 shallot, peeled and chopped

3 garlic cloves, smashed

½ cup chicken stock, preferably homemade (page 173), or low-sodium store-bought

1 cup cherries, fresh or frozen, halved and pitted

2 tablespoons cherry or berry whole-fruit preserves

2 teaspoons honey

1 teaspoon rosemary leaves, chopped

2 tablespoons fresh lemon juice

1 tablespoon unsalted butter

1 Preheat the oven to 300°F.

2 Rinse the duck inside and out, and pat dry. Trim excess fat from the neck and cavity, snip off wingtips, and discard. Mix 1 tablespoon salt and ½ teaspoon pepper in a small bowl, and season the bird inside and out. Using a paring knife, make dozens of slits through the skin and fat—taking care not to pierce the meat—all over both sides and all parts of the bird.

3 Put the duck breast side up on a rack in a roasting pan, and roast for 1 hour. Take the bird out of the oven, transfer to a platter, and carefully drain the fat from the pan into a measuring cup (you'll end up getting 2 to 3 cups). Return the duck to the pan, prick with the knife again, turn it breast side down, and roast another hour. Repeat each hour, roasting the duck for a total of 4½ hours.

4 While the duck cooks, make the sauce: In a small saucepan, heat 1 tablespoon duck fat over medium heat and cook the shallot until soft, about 4 minutes. Add the garlic and cook until fragrant, 1 minute. Add the stock, cherries, preserves, honey, and rosemary, and simmer until slightly thickened, about 10 minutes. Remove from the heat, add the lemon juice, swirl in the butter, and taste for salt and pepper. Set aside until the duck is finished.

(recipe continues)

Save that duck
fat! Use it to make
staggeringly
delicious potatoes
(page 93).

5 After 4½ hours of roasting, turn the oven temperature up to 350°F, prick the duck skin one last time, salt the skin again, and return the bird to the oven, breast side up. Roast for 30 minutes, until the skin is nicely browned.

6 Remove from the oven, tent with foil, and let rest for 20 minutes. Gently reheat the sauce over low heat. Carve the duck, put the pieces on a serving platter, and serve with the sauce.

Duck Ragù WITH HOMEMADE WHOLE-WHEAT FETTUCCINE SERVES 4

THIS DISH IS a guaranteed dinner-party home run. If you have a butcher who sells duck legs, definitely buy those; they're half the price of a breast. But I wrote this with breasts as an option because many supermarkets don't carry duck legs. And you could, of course, use store-bought noodles (I often do) or serve this with a different type of pasta (I'm very partial to farfalle, aka bowties). Or, you could make the pasta entirely with white flour—works exactly the same. But I like pairing this simple recipe for whole-wheat pasta with this sauce, in particular, because the pasta's heartiness works so well with the soulful, deeply flavorful sauce. This is one of my favorite dishes, especially on a cool night.

3 duck legs or 1 (1-pound) duck breast half

Kosher salt and freshly ground black pepper

½ cup chopped yellow onion

1 teaspoon chopped rosemary or thyme leaves

1 large garlic clove, chopped

⅛ teaspoon cayenne

1 teaspoon juniper berries (optional), crushed and tied in a cheesecloth sachet

⅔ cup dry red wine

2½ cups chicken stock, preferably homemade (page 173), or low-sodium store-bought

1 (15-ounce) can chopped tomatoes

½ pound Homemade Whole-Wheat Fettuccine (recipe follows)

1 If using duck legs, season them all over with salt and pepper and sear them in a sauté pan over medium-high heat until well browned on all sides, about 10 minutes.

2 If using a duck breast, make slashes all the way through the skin and fat (but not the meat) at ¼-inch intervals before seasoning both sides with salt and pepper. In a sauté pan, cook the breast skin side down over medium heat, draining the fat once, until golden brown, about 18 minutes. Turn the breast over and brown the other side for about 2 minutes.

3 Remove the duck (legs or breast) to a plate and drain off all but 2 tablespoons of fat from the pan. Add the onion to the pan and cook over medium heat for about 5 minutes. Then add the rosemary, garlic, cayenne, and juniper, if using, and sauté until fragrant, 1 minute. Add the wine and simmer for 4 minutes, scraping up brown bits. Add the stock, tomatoes and their juices, duck (if cooking a breast, put it skin side up), and 1 teaspoon salt, and bring to a boil. Reduce the heat, cover, and simmer, stirring occasionally, until very tender, about 45 minutes.

4 Transfer the duck to a plate and let it cool a little. Remove the skin and bones and discard. Shred the duck meat with your fingers.

(recipe continues)

5 Remove the juniper berries sachet. You can either return the duck meat to the liquid and serve as is, or, for a more elegant presentation and sauce that really clings to the noodles, puree the liquid first in a blender or food processor, and *then* add the meat. Be careful blending hot liquids; you may need to do it in batches.

6 Cook the pasta in boiling salted water until just shy of al dente, 2 to 5 minutes. Drain well. Add the noodles to the sauce, and simmer until the pasta is al dente. Divide among 4 large bowls and serve immediately.

Homemade Whole-Wheat Fettuccine MAKES ABOUT 1 POUND

This recipe makes twice as much pasta as needed for a recipe of duck ragù; freeze extra for up to a few months.

2 cups all-purpose flour

1 cup whole-wheat flour

1 teaspoon table salt

4 large eggs

1 tablespoon extra-virgin olive oil

1 Combine both flours and the salt in a food processor; pulse for 5 seconds to combine. Add the eggs and oil, and process until the dough starts to form a ball. If it doesn't come together, mix in 1 tablespoon water at a time until it does.

2 Turn the dough out onto a lightly floured surface, and knead for a minute or two, until it forms a smooth ball. Wrap in plastic wrap and let rest for at least 15 minutes, so that the gluten will relax and the dough will be easy to work.

3 Follow the directions on your pasta machine for rolling and cutting fettuccine, pappardelle, or another broad, flat noodle. Toss noodles with flour to keep them from sticking.

PAN-SEARED Duck Breasts
WITH FRESH PEACH COMPOTE SERVES 4

DUCK IS A RED-MEAT creature, and is terrific medium-rare. The breast, one of the more popular parts of most birds, is easy to cook, once you get the hang of it. Sizzle it slowly, skin side down, so that the enormous layer of fat beneath that skin melts and renders out, while the skin fries to crispy, ducky chicharrón. A duck breast half is usually about a pound, and can serve two people.

2 (16-ounce) duck breasts, rinsed and patted dry

Kosher salt and freshly ground black pepper

2 large peaches, peeled, pitted, and cut into large dice

¼ cup Triple Sec

2 tablespoons honey

1 teaspoon snipped chives

If peaches aren't in season, use one (10-ounce) bag frozen peach sections instead.

1 Using a sharp knife and cutting on the diagonal, score the skin and fat of the duck every ¼ inch without cutting into the meat. Season both sides of the duck with salt and pepper.

2 Heat a large sauté pan over medium-high heat, add the duck, skin side down, and reduce the heat to medium-low. Cook until nearly all the fat has rendered and the skin is crispy and golden brown, draining off the fat once, about 18 minutes.

3 While the duck is cooking, in a small saucepan, combine the peaches, Triple Sec, honey, and ½ teaspoon salt, and bring to a simmer over medium heat. Reduce the heat to low, and simmer until the fruit has softened and the sauce has thickened, about 8 minutes. Remove from the heat, stir in the chives, cover, and keep warm.

4 When the duck fat has rendered and the skin is golden, turn the breasts and cook for 2 or 3 minutes for medium-rare. Remove to a cutting board, skin side up, tent with foil, and let rest for 5 minutes.

5 Carve the duck into ¼-inch slices. Fan half of each breast onto a warmed plate, top with some compote, and serve immediately.

Modern Cassoulet SERVES 8 TO 12

IN THE INTRO to Julia Child's huge and definitive recipe for cassoulet, there is a section I find especially charming: "A Note on the Order of Battle." And what a battle it is: six solid pages of soaking, searing, and simmering, including the roasting of lamb bones, all to make a peasant stew. Julia advised that it is *possible* to make the dish in a day (!), but that it's much easier spread over two. Or *three*. Talk about a kitchen adventure!

My version of this beloved French classic is easily done with a couple of hours' work, is deeply flavorful, and is much lower in fat than the original. If you can cook a pot of chili, you can cook this—the techniques are the same: soak beans, brown meats, simmer until tender. And while that magic simmering is happening, flavor from the meats permeates the beans (and your house), along with herbs, aromatic vegetables, maybe a splash of red wine. Toss a simple salad and crack off a chunk of baguette. There is no more satisfying meal on a wintry day.

1 pound dried cannellini beans

Kosher salt and freshly ground black pepper

4 duck legs

4 garlic sausages, cut in 2-inch chunks

4 slices of bacon, diced

1 large yellow onion, chopped

2 medium carrots, chopped

2 celery ribs, chopped

5 garlic cloves, peeled and thinly sliced

1 tablespoon tomato paste

½ cup dry red wine

1 (15-ounce) can diced tomatoes

2 cups fresh, crusty bread in coarse chunks

1 tablespoon extra-virgin olive oil

1 scant tablespoon sweet paprika

¼ teaspoon cayenne

2 tablespoons flat-leaf parsley leaves

Canned beans are not an option here—they would turn to mush. If you forgot to soak your beans, quick-soak them: add enough cold water to come 2 inches above the beans, bring to a boil for 2 minutes, and let rest, covered, for 1 hour; drain and continue with recipe.

1 Soak the beans in 3 quarts of water for 6 hours. Drain.

2 Salt and pepper the duck legs all over. Then, over medium-high heat in a 6- to 8-quart Dutch oven, using a spatter screen on top, brown the duck legs well, about 12 minutes. Transfer to a plate, and pour off the fat from the pan. Reduce the heat to medium-low and gently brown, in turn, the sausages and bacon, rendering the fat. Add to the plate with the duck legs.

(recipe continues)

3 Preheat the oven to 350°F.

4 Remove all but 2 tablespoons fat from the pan, add the onion, carrots, and celery, and cook over medium heat until soft but not browned, about 8 minutes. Add 4 of the garlic cloves and cook until fragrant, 1 minute. Push the vegetables to the side, add the tomato paste, and toast it on the bottom of the pan for 2 minutes. Stir into the vegetables. Deglaze with the wine, scraping up the brown bits from the pan, and simmer until mostly evaporated.

5 Arrange the meats in the pan, add the tomatoes and their juices, the beans, and 5 cups water; the beans should be covered by about an inch of water. Bring to a simmer, cover, and bake at a gentle simmer until the beans are tender, 60 to 90 minutes, checking after 45 minutes to make sure the beans are still covered with liquid and adding more if needed. Taste and adjust the seasoning (it will likely need more salt).

6 Meanwhile, combine the bread chunks, remaining garlic clove, the olive oil, and 1/2 teaspoon salt in a food processor, and process into coarse bread crumbs (not powder). Add the paprika, cayenne, and parsley, and pulse a couple of times.

7 Evenly spread half of the bread crumb topping over the cassoulet, cover, and bake for 15 minutes; this helps to set the topping. Remove the lid, sprinkle the remaining topping over the cassoulet, and bake, uncovered, for 15 minutes. If the breading isn't browned enough, broil it for a minute. Serve, making sure each serving includes the crispy topping and a taste of each of the meats.

My version of this French classic is easily done in a couple of hours, and is much lighter than the original—but still rib-stickingly satisfying.

A BIT OF QUACK, A TOUCH OF OINK

On the meats involved in your cassoulet, it's entirely up to you. Different regions of France have traditionally used different products, depending on what animals were farmed locally. Generally, you want some duck or goose, some sausage, and some sort of salty pork. If you can find Toulouse-style garlic sausages, by all means, buy them; kielbasa, which even Julia considered a suitable variation, is my substitute of choice. Sweet Italian sausage isn't bad, although the fennel is a bit too pronounced. I use duck legs, available in most Asian markets, because they're delicious and much less pricey than breasts, but many American markets sell only breasts of duck. If that's your best option, buy just a single, 1-pound breast half, score the skin thoroughly, and render out the fat in a skillet over medium heat for about 20 minutes (straining and saving the fat). Then, remove the skin, shred the breast into small, bite-size pieces, and proceed. Finally, as regards pig, I use bacon because it's easy and available everywhere; you could instead use salt pork or a ham hock. Many recipes also call for cubes of lamb, pork loin, or pork shoulder. Your call—just be sure to brown everything thoroughly for flavor and color, and keep your meat total in the 2-pound range.

In a real pinch, you could even substitute chicken thighs for the duck—just don't serve it to French people.

Deconstructed Turkey
WITH SAGE GRAVY MAKES 8 TO 12 SERVINGS

AH, THE HOLIDAYS, when millions of people who never cook at all suddenly decide they should feed seventeen dishes to twenty-seven people—and that the focal point of the meal should be an enormous, odd-shaped bird they bought frozen solid. There's a reason we need an 800 number for talking turkey novices off the ledge—inevitably because they didn't thaw the thing properly, and didn't notice until showtime. Well, here's my solution: buy and cook your turkey in parts; that is, buy a bone-in breast, and as many drumsticks as you like.

There are plenty of reasons. A whole bird takes a week to thaw in the fridge, consuming an enormous amount of space when you need it most; parts, if frozen at all, thaw much faster. Because breast meat cooks faster than dark meat, having them detached from each other presents an obvious advantage: the breast will not be hideously overcooked and dry by the time the legs are ready. There's also no trussing, no stuffing, and your carving job is halfway done. You can respond to your family's preferences for more dark meat, more white meat, or none of either, as you wish. Finally, you can tell the children that this turkey had three legs.

TURKEY

⅓ cup kosher salt

¼ cup honey

1 head of garlic, cut in half (do not peel)

2 bay leaves

4 sprigs fresh thyme

4 large sprigs fresh sage, plus more for garnish

2 teaspoons black peppercorns

2 teaspoons allspice berries

¼ cup celery leaves (from 1 bunch)

1 (6½- to 7-pound) bone-in turkey breast

3 turkey drumsticks (about 2¼ pounds total)

2 turkey thighs (about 1½ pounds total)

3 tablespoons unsalted butter, melted

GRAVY

2 to 3 cups chicken stock, preferably homemade (page 173), or low-sodium store-bought

4 tablespoons (½ stick) unsalted butter

⅓ cup all-purpose flour

1 tablespoon chopped sage leaves

Kosher salt and freshly ground black pepper

You can brine the turkey as specified here, or you can skip that step and just rub the pieces with butter, salt, pepper, and herbs. But I highly recommend the salt bath; brining is the best thing ever to happen to turkey, producing moist meat that's seasoned through and through.

1 Brine the turkey: Pour 1 cup water into a small saucepan, add the salt and honey, and heat over high heat, stirring until dissolved. Remove from the heat, add the garlic, bay leaves, thyme, 2 of the sage sprigs, the peppercorns, allspice, and celery leaves, and let steep for a few minutes. Transfer to a 4-quart container and add a cup of ice cubes and 2½ quarts cold water, bringing the volume to 3 quarts.

2 Rinse the turkey parts, place in doubled 2½-gallon resealable plastic bags (or a large stockpot), and pour in the brine. Press out any air, close the bags, and place in a large bowl or other container to protect against leaks. Refrigerate for at least 6 hours or overnight.

3 To roast the turkey, arrange racks in the upper and lower thirds of the oven, and preheat the oven to 425°F.

4 Remove the turkey parts from the brine, pat dry with paper towels, and arrange, skin side up, on racks set in 2 medium roasting pans (be sure to leave space between the parts for air circulation). Pour 1 cup water into each pan. Drizzle the turkey parts with the melted butter. Pick the leaves from the remaining 2 sage sprigs, and scatter the leaves over the turkey. Put 1 pan on each oven rack and roast the turkey until it's beginning to brown, about 30 minutes.

5 Reduce the oven temperature to 400°F, switch the position of the pans, and rotate each pan 180 degrees. Continue roasting for 15 minutes, then check the temperature of the legs with an instant-read thermometer inserted into the thickest part of the meat; at 165°F, they're done. Check the breast, too; depending on the size differential, it could be done, or may need anywhere from 10 to 30 minutes more. Legs should take 1½ hours, and bone-in breast 2 to 3 hours. As they are ready, transfer the turkey parts to a platter and tent with foil.

(recipe continues)

After the gravy has thickened, reduce the heat to low to keep the gravy warm while you carve the turkey.

6 Make the gravy: Pour the pan juices into a 4-cup glass measuring cup, let stand until the fat rises to the top, 2 to 3 minutes, then skim off and discard the fat.

7 Set 1 roasting pan across 2 burners, add 2 cups chicken stock, and bring to a simmer over medium-high heat, scraping up any browned bits. Add the simmering stock to the pan juices in the measuring cup, then add additional chicken stock, if needed, to equal 4 cups liquid.

8 In a medium saucepan over medium-low heat, melt the butter, then whisk in the flour, and cook, whisking constantly, until smooth, approximately 2 minutes. Gradually whisk in the stock mixture and any collected juices from the platter holding the turkey, then raise the heat to medium-high and boil, uncovered, until the gravy is thickened, about 8 minutes.

9 Add the chopped sage, and season the gravy with salt and pepper. Carve turkey pieces and garnish with sage sprigs; serve with the gravy.

COINTREAU **Cranberry Relish** MAKES 3 CUPS

IN MY NEVER-ENDING quest to find new ways to debase healthy, innocent food with alcohol, more success! But, seriously, having added citrus zest to cranberries for a long time, I thought further amplification of the orange notes via liqueur would be lovely. A very subtle use of sweet spice and some texture and tartness from a Granny Smith apple lend still more interest, turning a compulsory holiday dish into something new.

1 (12-ounce) bag fresh cranberries

1 Granny Smith apple, peeled, cored, and diced

1 cup sugar

½ cup Cointreau or Grand Marnier orange liqueur

¼ teaspoon ground cinnamon

¼ teaspoon ground cloves

Grated zest of 1 lemon

Grated zest of 1 orange

In a medium saucepan over medium heat, combine the cranberries, apple, sugar, Cointreau, ½ cup water, the cinnamon, and cloves, and bring to a boil. Reduce the heat and simmer until the cranberries start to pop, about 10 minutes. Remove from the heat, stir in the zests, and chill.

Chestnut Stuffing SERVES 12

FOR ME, THIS IS the second-most important dish on the holiday table, almost edging out the turkey. It's so important to me that every year, I seem to forget what a bother it is to shell fresh chestnuts (ouch!), but what other time of year do you get to eat delicious roast chestnuts? They're worth it. This also provides an excellent place to use the turkey liver; it's definitely a background note, but I like it there. I guess I should call this dressing, because I never stuff my turkeys anymore, but some traditions die hard.

1 pound fresh chestnuts

8 cups coarse fresh bread crumbs, from crusty bread

4 cups diced cornbread

1 cup (2 sticks) unsalted butter, plus more for baking dish

1 extra-large yellow onion, chopped

2 celery ribs, chopped

1 turkey liver, cleaned and finely chopped

2 large eggs, lightly beaten

½ cup flat-leaf parsley leaves, chopped

¼ cup sage leaves, chopped

1 teaspoon kosher salt

¼ teaspoon freshly ground black pepper

1 cup chicken or turkey stock, preferably homemade (page 173), or low-sodium store-bought

1 Preheat the oven to 450°F.

2 Cut an X into the round end of each chestnut, place on a rimmed baking sheet, put in the oven, and add ¼ cup water to the pan. Roast for 10 minutes; the shells should peel back where cut. Remove from the oven, let cool a minute or two, and peel while the chestnuts are still warm. Chop coarsely.

3 Decrease the oven temperature to 350°F. Spread the bread crumbs on a baking sheet and bake until dry and golden, 15 minutes. Put in a large bowl with the chestnuts and cornbread.

4 In a large sauté pan over medium heat, melt the butter, then add the onion, celery, and chopped liver, and cook until the vegetables are soft, about 8 minutes. Add to the bowl with the chestnuts.

5 Stir in the eggs, parsley, sage, salt, pepper, and chicken stock. Spoon into a buttered 3-quart baking dish, and bake, covered, for 30 minutes. Uncover and bake for 30 minutes, until browned.

You can substitute dry-packed bottled chestnuts in a pinch; you'll need 7 ounces. But your house will not smell as good.

I like to leave the crust on the bread when making bread crumbs; it adds great crunch.

Grilled Chile-Lime Shrimp WITH ISRAELI COUSCOUS, MANGO, AND ZUCCHINI SERVES 4

SHRIMP ARE SUCH little flavor sponges; just a short plunge in this Caribbean-feeling marinade, and they become vivid, spicy, and bright. I love toothsome Israeli couscous, and toasting the little pearls takes these beads of pasta to a whole new level (see page 157). Pairing it with mango and zucchini, which I cut in big slices and grill before dicing, brings juicy sweetness to the party.

SHRIMP

- 1 teaspoon grated lime zest
- ¼ cup fresh lime juice
- 3 tablespoons extra-virgin olive oil
- 2 tablespoons low-sodium soy sauce
- 1 jalapeño chile, seeded and minced
- 2 tablespoons chopped cilantro leaves
- 1 tablespoon minced garlic
- 1 tablespoon sugar
- 1 teaspoon chili powder
- ¼ teaspoon cayenne
- 1½ pounds medium shrimp in the shell

COUSCOUS

- 2 cups Israeli couscous
- 1 mango
- 1 medium zucchini
- Vegetable oil, for brushing
- 2½ cups chicken stock, preferably homemade (page 173), or low-sodium store-bought
- ½ to 1 teaspoon kosher salt, to taste
- 1 tablespoon unsalted butter
- 2 tablespoons chopped flat-leaf parsley leaves

Be sure not to marinate the shrimp for more than 30 minutes, or the lime juice will turn them to ceviche; then, when you grill, you'll turn them into rubber.

1 Marinate the shrimp: In a medium bowl, stir together the lime zest, juice, olive oil, soy, jalapeño, cilantro, garlic, sugar, chili powder, and cayenne. Peel the shrimp, leaving on the tails, and devein.

2 Rinse, and then pat completely dry with paper towels. Put the shrimp in a large zipper bag, pour the marinade over, close the bag, pushing out any air, and rub the marinade into the shrimp. Refrigerate for 20 minutes.

(recipe continues)

If using wooden skewers, make sure to soak them in water for 30 minutes before using to prevent them from burning on the grill.

3 Preheat a grill to medium-high.

4 Make the couscous: In a dry, medium saucepan over medium-low heat, toast the couscous, stirring frequently, until golden brown, 8 to 10 minutes. Set aside.

5 Peel the mango, stand it on its end with a skinny edge facing you, and run your knife close to the seed core to cut 2 slices off each of the two sides, making 4 slices each ½ inch thick. (Eat the remaining mango for a snack.) Slice the zucchini lengthwise into ⅓- to ½-inch slices.

6 Brush the mango and zucchini pieces with vegetable oil on both sides and grill until charred and tender, 6 to 8 minutes. Let cool, and then cut into ½-inch chunks.

7 In a medium saucepan, bring the chicken stock to a boil. Add the toasted couscous, stir, cover, reduce the heat, and simmer for 7 minutes. Add the mango, zucchini, ½ teaspoon salt, the butter, and parsley; cook for 1 minute. Taste for seasoning and doneness. Keep warm.

8 Put the shrimp on a cutting board and nestle them together in groups of 6. Using 2 skewers for each group (this keeps them from falling into the grill and makes them easier to turn), skewer the shrimp. Grill the shrimp until just cooked through, 2 minutes per side, and serve on top of the couscous.

A TOAST TO TOASTING

There is a famous joint in NYC called Murray's Bagels that, citing tradition, refuses to toast a bagel, even if you beg them to. As such, I probably won't be going to Murray's Bagels. To me, an untoasted bagel tastes gummy and raw, while a toasted one gets golden brown and crispy on the outside, and softer and warm on the inside.

Toasting—that is, carefully dry-cooking food over fairly high heat until just the moment before it begins to burn—produces some of the most aromatic and irresistible golden brown flavor notes there are, and changes texture, too. I think it's almost as magical and elemental as the effect that seasoning with salt has on foods. Toasting raw nuts in a dry skillet develops flavor, color, and crunch; ditto sesame seeds and pine nuts. For me, toasted bread is mandatory for sandwiches and for serving alongside soup. Toasting pasta makes it nutty tasting and sometimes, as in the case of pearl couscous, gives it a nice toothsome texture.

Just be careful and don't try to multitask when dry-toasting in a skillet or oven—probably about half the time I do this, I step away to take a phone call and the kitchen fills with smoke. Stand still. Stir as needed. You'll be done in a few minutes, and it will be entirely worth the trouble.

Indian chefs not only always start with whole spices and grind them fresh but they also toast or fry them before using to really bring out their flavors and aromas (often called "blooming" the spices).

Scampi Skewers WITH LEMON ZUCCHINI

SERVES 4 AS AN APPETIZER OR LIGHT LUNCH

GARLIC, BUTTER, AND lemon are, of course, a holy trinity for shrimp—everybody loves the combination. But my favorite thing about this dish is its use of the humble zucchini: uncooked, cut paper-thin, wilted slightly by a short bath in lemon vinaigrette, then beautifully arranged beneath a skewer full of shrimp.

ZUCCHINI

2 medium zucchini

3 tablespoons extra-virgin olive oil

Grated zest of 1 lemon

1 tablespoon fresh lemon juice

¼ teaspoon sugar

¼ teaspoon fine sea salt

Pinch of freshly ground black pepper

SHRIMP

½ cup panko or dried coarse baguette bread crumbs

8 tablespoons (1 stick) unsalted butter, at room temperature

1 large egg yolk

2 garlic cloves, minced

1 teaspoon grated lemon zest

1½ tablespoons fresh lemon juice

1½ tablespoons dry white wine

1 tablespoon finely chopped basil leaves

1 tablespoon finely chopped flat-leaf parsley leaves

¾ teaspoon kosher salt

1 pound medium shrimp, peeled and deveined, tails on

Both the zucchini base and the skewers are great for prepping a couple of hours before company comes; cover them and keep them chilled.

1 Prepare the zucchini: Trim the ends from the zucchini so that the zucchini fit the plates you intend to use. Using a mandoline or vegetable peeler, cut the zucchini into paper-thin slices and stack them flat (don't pile them in curls in a bowl, or they'll stay curly). Arrange 6 to 9 slices on each of 4 plates in rows or a basket weave pattern. Reserve leftover zucchini for another use (or do what I do: hit them with salt and pop them in your mouth).

2 Whisk together the olive oil, lemon zest, lemon juice, sugar, salt, and pepper. Drizzle the vinaigrette over the zucchini, and set aside for at least 15 minutes to soften and flavor the zucchini.

(recipe continues)

This dish is equally good when the shrimp are replaced by seared scallops, a fillet of mild fish, or any number of other things.

3   Meanwhile, prepare the shrimp: Preheat the oven to 425°F.

4   In a small bowl, combine the panko, butter, egg, garlic, lemon zest, lemon juice, wine, basil, parsley, and salt.

5   Place 2 shrimp on a cutting board, nestled tail to body, forming a yin-yang design, and thread onto a skewer. Repeat with two more pairs of shrimp, 6 shrimp per skewer. Trim the skewers with scissors if necessary to fit on the serving plates.

6   Put the shrimp in a baking dish. Cover with the butter mixture, dotting it on top. Bake until the shrimp are pink and just cooked through, 10 to 12 minutes.

7   Place one shrimp skewer atop each plate of zucchini salad, and serve.

Spicy Mussels IN GREEN CURRY SERVES 4

FEW THINGS LOOK more gorgeous on the table than a steaming bowl of shiny black mussels, and it's hard to find a more fun, tongue-tingling way to eat. Aside from the plump mollusks, my favorite part about the dish is sopping up the vivid, spicy broth with garlic toast—an accompaniment that would seem to make little sense given the Thai flavors involved. Until you're doing it. But if this sort of culinary fusion makes you feel dirty, serve the mussels over hot, steamed rice instead.

TOASTS

1 crusty baguette, sliced ⅓ inch thick on the diagonal

½ cup extra-virgin olive oil

1 large garlic clove, peeled and cut in half

Kosher salt

CURRY PASTE

6 tablespoons chopped tender lemongrass stalk

3 green Thai bird chiles or 1 jalapeño, coarsely chopped

2 poblano chiles, seeded

3 small shallots, coarsely chopped

3 large garlic cloves, coarsely chopped

1 (2-inch) piece of fresh ginger, peeled and coarsely chopped

¼ cup chopped cilantro leaves and stems

2 kaffir lime leaves, coarsely chopped, or grated zest of 2 limes

½ teaspoon ground cumin

½ teaspoon ground coriander

3 tablespoons fish sauce

1 teaspoon honey

MUSSELS

1 tablespoon vegetable oil

1 medium yellow onion, halved and sliced

3 cups trimmed and snapped Chinese long beans or green beans

1 (13.5-ounce) can coconut milk

2 pounds mussels, scrubbed, beards removed; any cracked or open mussels discarded

2 tablespoons fresh lime juice

2 tablespoons chopped cilantro leaves

2 tablespoons chopped basil leaves, preferably Thai

1 Heat a grill or grill pan over high heat.

2 Make the toasts: Brush the bread slices with the oil and grill until golden and crispy, about 2 minutes per side. Rub one side with the garlic clove and sprinkle with salt. Set aside.

(recipe continues)

If you're unsure how powerful your chiles are, start by adding only a small amount of them; you can always *add* heat to the broth later, but good luck removing it.

3 Make the curry paste: Combine the lemongrass, both types of chile, shallots, garlic, ginger, cilantro, kaffir lime, cumin, coriander, fish sauce, and honey in the bowl of a food processor and process until a smooth paste is formed, 20 to 30 seconds.

4 Cook the mussels: Put a large pot over medium-high heat and add the oil and onion. Cook the onion until it starts to brown, about 5 minutes. Add the curry paste to the onion and cook until it becomes fragrant, about 2 minutes, then add the green beans, and stir to combine. Next add the coconut milk, reduce the heat to medium-low, and cook for 5 minutes to combine the flavors.

5 Add the mussels to the pot, increase the heat back to medium-high, cover, and cook until the mussels open, 5 to 7 minutes. Add the lime juice, cilantro, and basil, stir to combine, and serve immediately with the toasts for sopping up the broth.

Scallops and Cheddar Grits

THE FIRST TIME I had the Southern classic shrimp and grits was on set during the filming of *Top Chef* in Miami, brilliantly prepared by Dallas-based chef Tre Wilcox in a taco truck. I've been hooked ever since. Here, the same idea, but with sea scallops— also a sweet shellfish, and one that needs no peeling or deveining. Scallops are particularly friendly with salty, spicy pork, whether it's fancy Italian ham, good old bacon, or, in this case, the spicy Spanish sausage that rounds out this dish.

Kosher salt

¾ cup grits

6 ounces sharp Cheddar cheese, grated (1½ cups)

16 sea scallops, trimmed of tough muscle flap (if present)

1 tablespoon extra-virgin olive oil

1 link (about 4 ounces) cooked, Spanish-style chorizo, casing removed, cut into matchsticks or just crumbled

½ cup finely chopped scallions (white and green parts)

1 garlic clove, finely chopped

1 tablespoon fresh lemon juice

1 Preheat the oven to its lowest temperature (usually 170°F) for warming.

2 In a medium saucepan over high heat, bring 3½ cups water to a boil, and add ¼ teaspoon salt. Slowly stir the grits into the water, pouring the grits in a fine stream. Reduce the heat, cover, and simmer until thickened, 15 to 20 minutes. Stir in the Cheddar, cover, and keep warm in the oven.

Always insist upon "dry" scallops. "Wet" scallops have been soaked in sodium tripolyphosphate, which gives them a longer shelf life by helping them retain excess moisture—and which, accordingly, makes them hard to brown and obscures their sweet flavor. Also, before cooking, check scallops for any residual bits of connective muscle, which looks like a little flap on the side of the cylindrical critter; it is almost always left attached to the yummy part, and it is inedibly tough.

3 Ten minutes into cooking the grits, pat dry the scallops, season them with salt on both sides, and heat a sauté pan over medium-high heat. Add the olive oil to the pan, then the chorizo, and cook until the sausage renders some fat, 2 to 3 minutes. Add the scallops, shake the pan to move them around a little, and sear for 2 minutes. Turn and continue cooking until browned, 2 minutes. Remove the scallops to a plate lined with a paper towel, and place in the oven. Keep the chorizo in the pan.

4 Reduce the heat under the pan to medium, and add the scallions, garlic, and lemon juice. Cook for 2 minutes, and remove from the heat.

5 On each of 4 plates, make a bed of grits, then place the scallops on top, and drizzle pan sauce and chorizo on and around the scallops and grits. Serve quickly.

ADDLED VALUE

Here's a worthwhile discovery that you can apply pretty much throughout the grocery store: most products labeled "quick" or "instant" are barely any faster than the real thing; invariably have been packed with weird, bad-tasting, science-y ingredients; and always cost more money. This kind of stuff is invented because there aren't many ways for food companies to increase their profit on the sale of, say, an apple. They have to add value to that apple. So they slice half an apple, sprinkle it with a preservative, and seal it in a single-serving bag: Voilà! A ready-packed snack to sell for easily twice the price of a humble piece of fruit, and with a shelf life of months and the opportunity to emblazon a colorful brand logo on a piece of plastic packaging. All of which is to say, creepy. For me, real food, please.

Fried Rice WITH CRAB, GREENS, AND HAPPY EGGS SERVES 4

TO ME, THIS READS like an off-duty chef's late-night stoner food—leftover rice from Chinese takeout, canned crab from the pantry, a cheerful, gooey fried egg on top. In any case, this is a superb use for the excess containers of rice we always have from Kum Kau down the block. If you don't have any, bake your own (see page 91) and come back. And if you're planning ahead to cook this, consider swinging by a gourmet market for some tiny quail eggs, which are even happier looking.

¼ cup fish sauce

5 Thai bird chiles, thinly sliced

1 garlic clove, minced

1 tablespoon fresh lime juice, plus 2 limes, cut into wedges, for serving

4 tablespoons vegetable oil

6 large eggs

Kosher salt and freshly ground black pepper

4 cups cooked rice, cold

1 cup thinly sliced scallion (white and green parts)

1 pound jumbo lump crabmeat, canned or fresh, gently picked over to remove shells, but kept in large pieces

1 cup roughly chopped cooked greens, such as spinach, Swiss chard, or mustard greens

2 garlic cloves, chopped

3 tablespoons soy sauce

½ teaspoon sugar

2 tablespoons chopped cilantro leaves

1 In a small bowl, mix together the fish sauce, chiles, minced garlic, lime juice, and 1 tablespoon water.

2 Heat a sauté pan over medium heat for 5 minutes. Add 1 tablespoon of the vegetable oil, and fry 4 of the eggs, sunny side up, about 5 minutes. Season with salt and pepper. Remove to a plate and keep warm in the oven turned on to its lowest temperature.

3 Put a large wok over medium-high heat and add the remaining 3 tablespoons oil. When hot and almost smoking, add the rice and the scallion, and stir to coat with the oil. Make a hole in the middle of the rice, and add the remaining 2 eggs, scrambling in the wok and stirring them to combine with the rice.

4 Add the crabmeat and the greens, and mix them in gently so as to not break up the lump crab. Add the chopped garlic, soy, sugar, and ½ teaspoon salt. Sprinkle with the cilantro and serve, putting a fried egg on top of each portion and passing the fish sauce mixture and lime wedges at the table.

Risotto WITH SHRIMP AND BAY SCALLOPS SERVES 4

THERE IS A MYTH that risotto requires constant attention and labor at the stove—it actually does not. Regular stirring will do. And it's easy to learn how to nibble rice kernels as you go until you've achieved al-dente perfection. For me, there are several more subtle issues: timing your cooking so the dish ends up loose and creamy, not tight and dry; using appropriately scanty amounts of meat and vegetables, because, just as I believe pizza is about the flatbread, risotto—the Italian word for "rice"—is about the rice; and, simply, using rich, delicious stock. The fact is, most grocery-store stock tastes like thin, salty water (my favorite exception is Kitchen Basics), but fortunately, even if you don't have a big pot of real fish stock from heads and tails and vegetables, it's easy and very effective to enrich commercial seafood stock by simmering the shells from lobster, shrimp, or crab for just a short time; there is a lot of fresh flavor and aroma there. This dish is light, creamy without cream, and fabulous.

8 cups seafood stock, preferably homemade (page 173), or low-sodium store-bought

½ pound medium shrimp, shelled (shells reserved), deveined, and cut in thirds crosswise

3 tablespoons extra-virgin olive oil

1 medium yellow onion, chopped

1 garlic clove, minced

1½ cups Arborio rice

½ cup dry white wine

½ pound bay scallops

¼ cup flat-leaf parsley leaves, chopped

1 Meyer lemon, zested and segmented (see page 64)

1 In a medium saucepan, bring the stock and reserved shells to a simmer, remove from the heat, cover, and let steep while you gather and prepare the other ingredients. Strain, discarding the solids, return the stock to the pan, and bring back to a gentle simmer over low heat. Cover partially.

2 In a large saucepan or Dutch oven, heat 2 tablespoons of the olive oil over medium heat. Add the onion, and sauté until soft and translucent, about 8 minutes. Add the garlic and cook until fragrant, 1 minute. Add the rice, stir well, and cook, stirring occasionally, for 3 minutes. Add the wine, stir, and simmer until it is almost completely absorbed by the rice.

3 Check your watch, and, stirring often, start adding the warmed broth with a ladle, half a cup at a time, letting the rice absorb each ladleful before adding another. After 15 minutes, start tasting the rice to get a feel for its doneness—you want it cooked through but not mushy; it should take about 18 minutes total.

4 While the rice cooks, heat the remaining tablespoon olive oil in a sauté pan over medium heat. Add the scallops and parcook for just 1 minute; reserve, along with any juices. Do the same with the shrimp.

5 When the rice is almost cooked, add the seafood, and cook for 1 minute. The risotto should be soft and soupy; add stock or water as needed. Remove from the heat, add the parsley and lemon zest, and serve immediately, topping each portion with a few lemon segments.

Pasta Primavera WITH PROSCIUTTO, ASPARAGUS, AND CARROTS SERVES 6

THIS IS THE QUINTESSENTIAL spring luncheon dish, all about the sweetness that's finally bursting up in gardens—long-awaited asparagus, shallot, and carrot—made rich with sweet cream. It's also about the way that sweetness seems more pronounced against the salty ham and the tangy mustard.

Kosher salt

1 pound penne or farfalle

1 pound medium asparagus spears, stems trimmed, cut into 1½-inch lengths

1 large carrot, cut into matchsticks

1 tablespoon extra-virgin olive oil

8 ounces sliced prosciutto, *jamón ibérico,* or other high-quality ham, cut into bite-size pieces

1 large shallot, sliced ⅛ inch thick

1 garlic clove, minced

½ teaspoon red pepper flakes

1 cup heavy cream

1 cup chicken stock, preferably homemade (page 173), or low-sodium store-bought

2 tablespoons Dijon mustard

1 Bring a pot of water to a boil, salt it generously, and (for an 11-minute penne, say) cook the pasta for 8 minutes, add the asparagus and carrots and cook for 3 minutes. Check the pasta and vegetables to make sure they're cooked through but still have texture, then drain.

2 While the pasta is cooking, heat the olive oil in a large sauté pan over medium heat, add the ham and shallot, and cook until lightly browned, 3 minutes or so. Add the garlic and pepper flakes and cook until fragrant, 1 minute. Add the cream, stock, and mustard, and simmer for a minute or two, scraping up any brown bits.

3 Add the pasta and vegetables to the pan. Toss and cook for another 2 minutes, until cooked through and the pasta is coated. Taste for seasoning, add salt if necessary, and serve immediately in warm bowls.

Pan-Roasted Cod IN BRODO SERVES 4

THIS RECIPE WAS inspired by Eric Ripert, the brilliant chef at Le Bernardin in New York City (to whom I am in no way comparing myself as a cook, let me be clear). One of his many incredible dishes is a crispy black bass fillet on braised celery with a sauce of veal stock, *ibérico* ham, and green peppercorns—yes, fish served in a beef broth that's been enriched with ham, wine, and spices, and reduced to further intensify it. This is a classic idea in French cooking, and it's simple and delicious.

1 shallot, chopped

2 ounces pancetta, chopped

3 tablespoons extra-virgin olive oil

1 small garlic clove, chopped

1 quart beef stock, preferably homemade (page 173), or low-sodium store-bought

½ teaspoon thyme leaves

1 tablespoon unsalted butter

Kosher salt and freshly ground black pepper

4 (6- to 8-ounce) skin-on cod fillets, the same size and thickness

Wondra or all-purpose flour, for dusting

2 teaspoons grated lemon zest

1 Preheat the oven to 425°F.

2 In a medium saucepan over medium heat, cook the shallot and pancetta in 1 tablespoon of the olive oil until the shallot is soft and the fat is somewhat rendered from the pancetta, about 8 minutes. Add the garlic and cook until fragrant, 1 minute. Add the stock and thyme, bring to a boil, reduce the heat, and simmer briskly until reduced by half to 2 cups, about 25 minutes. Strain, discarding the solids, and return the sauce to the pan. Swirl in the butter to melt, taste, and add salt and pepper as needed. Keep warm.

3 When the sauce is about halfway reduced, begin the fish: Heat an ovenproof sauté pan over medium-high heat for a good 5 minutes. Sprinkle each side of the fish with salt and pepper, and dust lightly with flour, shaking off excess. When the pan is heated, add the remaining 2 tablespoons oil, and then add the fish, skin-side down, sliding the fillets around for a moment to ensure they don't stick. Cook until the skin is crispy and golden, about 3 minutes.

4 Turn over the fillets, and transfer to the oven until just cooked through, 7 to 10 minutes.

5 Put each fillet in a wide, shallow bowl, drizzle broth around until the fish is about half-submerged. Garnish the fish with lemon zest and serve immediately.

THE STOCK MARKET

Clearly, considering the number of brands of new stocks and broths on store shelves, there is a lot of money to be made selling stock. Home cooks everywhere appear to have gotten the message that using stock instead of just water produces tastier rice, potatoes, and sauces, without adding fat.

But the reason those stocks improve food is mainly that they're contributing salt to it. Most store-bought stocks are little more than salty water with precious little meatiness or flavor from vegetables or herbs; it's not hard to see why it's profitable to sell salty water for $4 a quart. A recent ad campaign for the Swanson brand of broths cleverly bragged that theirs was the only major supermarket brand that does not contain MSG; the reason so many stocks *do* contain the much-maligned ingredient is that it makes food taste meatier than it is. And they need that boost of meatiness. If you look at the nutrition labels, most commercial stocks, including Swanson's, contain only 1 to 3 grams of protein per 1-cup serving.

For these reasons, I strongly encourage you to make your own chicken stock, at the very least. If you ever cook chickens, just freeze the carcasses until you have time. It's easy, it saves money, it's a great way to clean out the fridge and make use of withered veggies in your crisper. And the culinary payoff is huge. I make stock in large batches, and freeze it in pint containers. They thaw in the microwave in exactly five minutes.

For those times you must resort to store-bought, the next best option is a hand-crafted stock from a local butcher or gourmet shop that you trust or a high-quality concentrate like D'Artagnan's veal demi-glace (www.dartagnan.com). Among commercial grocery-store stocks, the only brand I like is Kitchen Basics, because it tastes beefy. Why? They actually use a decent amount of beef bones, and it's not excessively watered down. A one-cup serving of KB beef stock contains 5 grams of protein. To their enormous credit, they even sell completely salt-free stocks (for serious reducing).

Shrimp and lobster lend themselves to easily made and very flavorful stock; their shells, when sautéed with a little olive oil and onion, then simmered with celery and herbs, produce great aroma and flavor.

BELOW, THE BASIC STOCKS

You can add other veggies, herbs, or, if you like, garlic. I prefer to keep them simple and versatile. After simmering, strain, skim off fat, and refrigerate for a few days or freeze for months.

Chicken Stock: The mainstay. Throw the carcass from a roast chicken in a pot with an onion, quartered, a couple of celery ribs, a chopped carrot, a bay leaf, 6 peppercorns, 1 teaspoon salt, and enough water to cover everything; simmer for 1½ to 3 hours (longer is better), skimming off foam at the beginning.

Seafood Stock: Same ingredients as for chicken stock, but substitute 2 pounds fish bones, heads, and tails, and any available lobster or shrimp shells for the chicken carcass, and simmer for only 30 minutes.

Beef Stock: A little more trouble, because you have to make the effort to buy beef bones, and you have to roast them. But if you do, you'll be rewarded. First, preheat your oven to 450°F. Toss 4 pounds or so of beef shank bones with a chopped carrot and a couple of quartered onions in a deep roasting pan with olive oil, and roast until well browned, about 1 hour. Then cover with water, add a couple celery ribs, a bay leaf, some thyme sprigs, and a couple teaspoons salt, and simmer gently, skimming off foam at the beginning, for 4 hours.

Vegetable Stock: Make veggie stock when the fridge needs to be cleaned out; celery that has lost its crispiness is still perfectly fine for this use. Many cooks also save all of their veggie peelings in the freezer until stock time—a very thrifty and green idea. On a baking sheet or two, toss with olive oil a pound of quartered, unpeeled onions, a pound of chopped carrots, ½ pound of wild mushrooms, 3 garlic cloves, a chopped bell pepper (orange, red, or yellow), and 4 celery ribs, and roast at 400°F for 45 minutes. Scrape the veggies into a stockpot along with 1 chopped tomato, a bay leaf, a sprig of thyme, a handful of parsley, 6 peppercorns, and 2 teaspoons kosher salt. Cover with water and gently simmer for 1 hour.

Whole Striped Bass BAKED IN SALT CRUST

SERVES 4

THIS ANCIENT TECHNIQUE is easy, produces an impressive presentation, and results in the most lush, juicy fish you've ever tasted. The salt crust traps moisture, allowing the fish to steam in its own juices along with the aromas of lemons and herbs. The skin keeps the salt from getting to the meat. Striped bass is a great fish, sort of a cross between flaky and steaky; this technique also works well with red snapper, porgy, grouper, or branzino. The only thing that might be a little tricky for a first-timer, here, is filleting the fish to get the flesh off the bones. Don't worry—when food tastes this good, it doesn't need to look perfect!

4 cups kosher salt

6 large egg whites

4 sprigs of thyme, tarragon, or rosemary

1 (5-pound) striped bass or other fish, gutted, scaled, rinsed, and patted dry

4 thin slices of lemon

2 garlic cloves, smashed

1 bay leaf

You can try this technique with a smaller fish for two, or with a whole salmon for a crowd, scaling the crust up or down as needed.

Experiment with salt-crusted vegetables, such as beets and potatoes, or beef tenderloin.

1 Preheat the oven to 400°F.

2 Line a large baking sheet with foil (otherwise, the egg/salt mixture will all but ruin the pan). In a large bowl, stir together the salt and egg whites until evenly mixed.

3 Stuff the herbs inside the cavity of the fish, along with the lemon slices, garlic, and bay leaf.

4 Make a thin layer of salt crust in the pan large enough to accommodate the fish. Put the fish on top, and pack salt on and around it (some cooks like to keep the head visible, while others prefer to hide it; consider the tenderness of your guests' sensibilities when deciding). Bake for 30 to 40 minutes or until an instant-read thermometer reads 135°F in the thickest part of the fish (punch the probe right through the crust). Remove the fish from the oven and let it rest for 10 minutes.

5 To serve, with a sharp knife, make a horizontal cut in the side of the crust from nose to tail. Using a large fork or tongs, you should be able to lift the crust off in more or less one piece. You also can crack it with a utensil. Using the fork or a knife, gently scrape away the skin (it will come right off); then, using a fish spatula, gently lift out the first fillet, trying not to bring along bones. The second fillet is easier; grab the fish by the tail, and the bones, spine, and head should lift right off, leaving an intact, boneless fillet. Serve immediately.

THREE-FISH **Bouillabaisse** SERVES 4

WHILE MOST BOUILLABAISSE recipes contain easily six or more types of seafood—originally whatever a fisherman had left over at the end of the day—that's not really necessary. For my money, you really just need lobster, a firm fish, and either mussels or clams. Here, the flavorful broth is made entirely from the lobster shells, aromatics, and white wine; no store-bought stocks were used to debase the fresh, real ingredients here.

3 tablespoons extra-virgin olive oil

1 medium yellow onion, coarsely chopped, skins included for color

1 celery rib, chopped

1 medium carrot, chopped, plus 2 carrots, cut into ½-inch chunks

4 garlic cloves, smashed, plus 2 cloves, chopped

3 sprigs of thyme

1 bay leaf

6 black peppercorns

5 coriander seeds

⅛ teaspoon fennel seeds

1 cup dry white wine

Kosher salt

2 (1½- to 2-pound) live lobsters

1 medium leek, white and light green parts, chopped and well washed

2 small Yukon gold potatoes, peeled and cut in ½-inch chunks

½ fennel bulb, cut into matchsticks (reserve some fronds for garnish)

1 (28-ounce) can chopped Italian tomatoes, drained

2 large pinches of saffron

Grated zest of ½ orange

1 pound fresh halibut, flounder, hake, cod, sole—whatever white-fleshed fish is freshest and is sustainable

1 (2-pound) bag fresh mussels, washed and bearded; discard any with open or broken shells

1 tablespoon chopped flat-leaf parsley leaves

Be sure to serve with grilled crusty toasts to soak up the soup—or, better yet, use garlic bread.

1. In a large stockpot, heat the olive oil over medium heat. Add the onion, celery, and 1 chopped carrot; sauté until soft, about 7 minutes. Add the 4 smashed garlic cloves, the thyme, bay leaf, peppercorns, coriander, and fennel seeds, and sauté until fragrant, about 1 minute. Add the wine and simmer for 2 minutes. Add 2½ quarts water and 1 teaspoon salt, and bring to a boil over high heat.

2. Put the lobsters in the pot, cover, reduce the heat to medium, and boil for 12 minutes. Remove the lobsters (reserve the pot and cooking liquid), cool to room temperature, and shell all of the meat except from the claws, reserving the claws for presentation. Clean the vein from the tail section, cut the meat into bite-size pieces, and refrigerate.

3. Return the shells to the stockpot, bring to a boil, reduce the heat, and simmer for 40 minutes. Strain the broth through a China cap (see page 83) or a few layers of cheesecloth, discard the solids, and measure the liquid. You need 1½ quarts, at most, for 4 servings; if you have more broth than that, return to a boil in the stockpot and reduce. Season to taste with salt.

4. Add to the stockpot the diced carrots, the 2 chopped garlic cloves, the leek, potatoes, fennel, tomatoes, saffron, and orange zest, and cook until the vegetables are tender, about 20 minutes. Add the fish and mussels, cover, and cook until the fish is just firm and the mussels have opened (discard any that do not), about 8 minutes.

5. Return the lobster to the pot for 1 minute to heat through. Stir in the parsley, season with salt, if needed, and serve immediately, garnishing each bowl with one lobster claw.

Crispy Salmon WITH HORSERADISH AÏOLI SERVES 4

THIS RECIPE IS all about how to make fish skin crispy and delicious, the joy of homemade mayonnaise, and the necessity of fresh horseradish.

When it's soggy, the skin on a fish fillet is deeply unappetizing. But a fine coating of flour and careful panfrying can transform that skin into a deliciously salty, crispy chip, instantly making it the best part of the dish. Meanwhile, I don't know why some people fear making mayonnaise at home; a food processor renders it foolproof, and the addition of real, fresh horseradish root gives it amazing kick, flavor, and aroma. The bottled prepared stuff doesn't even come close.

AÏOLI

- 2 large egg yolks
- ¼ teaspoon kosher salt
- ½ cup canola oil
- ½ cup extra-virgin olive oil
- 1 tablespoon plus 1 teaspoon fresh lemon juice
- ½ teaspoon Worcestershire sauce
- 2 tablespoons finely grated peeled fresh horseradish root, to taste
- 1 tablespoon chopped flat-leaf parsley leaves

FISH

- 4 (8-ounce) skin-on salmon fillets of even thickness (preferably at least 1½ inches)
- Fine sea salt
- Wondra or all-purpose flour, for dusting
- 2 tablespoons canola oil

Wondra flour deserves its name. A very fine flour often used as a thickening agent in home kitchens, it is used in professional kitchens to give fish and seafood (think scallops) a thin crunchy crust. You can find it at well-stocked supermarkets.

The sauce is best made at least an hour or two before serving, so that the flavors can blend and develop in the fridge. In a pinch, you could fake the aïoli with a cup of store-bought mayonnaise, and just add the lemon juice, Worcestershire, horseradish, and parsley. But you won't know what you're missing!

1. Make the aïoli: Put the egg yolks, salt, and 1 tablespoon water in a food processor with the metal blade. With the motor running, slowly drizzle in both oils, and voilà!: mayonnaise. Add the lemon juice, Worcestershire, horseradish, and parsley, and pulse a couple of times to blend. Cover and refrigerate until serving.

2. Preheat the oven to 400°F.

3. Heat a 12-inch ovenproof sauté pan over medium heat until hot—at least 5 minutes. While the pan heats, pat dry the fillets with a paper towel, season on both sides with salt, and dust the skin side with a fine coating of flour. When the pan is ready (you should feel strong heat when you hold your hand a couple inches above it), add the oil and swirl it around the pan; place the fillets in the oil, skin-side down. Quickly give the pan a strong shake to move the fish around a bit; this prevents sticking. A few seconds later, give the pan another shake. Cook until golden brown, 3 minutes. Turn over the fish and put the pan in the oven. Cook for 6 to 8 minutes, until just cooked through.

4. Serve the fish on warm plates accompanied by a good dollop of aïoli.

THE FISH SPATULA

Once in a while, a simple tool comes along and changes your life—the kind that makes you wonder why nobody ever told you about it sooner. So I'm telling you now: get a fish spatula (sometimes called by the brand name Peltex in pro kitchens), and not just for fish. In fact, you will use it for everything. You know that moment when you want to dig that first brownie out of the pan, or that first slab of lasagna? That's when you need a fish spatula. It is thin and flexible stainless steel; the blade is angled and has just the right curve; and it's perforated so it's less inclined to stick to the food.

THE ULTIMATE NOT-PEPPERONI AND MUSHROOM Pizza
MAKES 2 (14-INCH) PIES; SERVES 4

MY GO-TO PIZZA is a classic, thin-crust margherita—which is just red sauce, fresh mozzarella, and basil—bastardized with pepperoni and mushrooms. Here is the result of my quest for the ultimate expression of my favorite pie, using genuine Italian salumi instead of factory pepperoni, amping up flavor with a good provolone and wild mushrooms, and making the sauce mouthwateringly piquant with a spike of red wine vinegar. Best of all, a crispy, tender crust with a very special ingredient (see page 184).

DOUGH

- 3 cups "00" Italian-style pizza flour, or all-purpose or bread flour, plus more for kneading
- 2 teaspoons kosher salt
- 1 teaspoon active dry yeast
- 2 tablespoons extra-virgin olive oil, plus more for bowl
- 1 cup warm water, or more if needed
- Cornmeal, as needed

SAUCE

- 1 (28-ounce) can San Marzano tomatoes
- 3 tablespoons extra-virgin olive oil
- 1 shallot, finely diced
- 1 tablespoon minced garlic
- 1½ teaspoons red wine vinegar
- 1 teaspoon sugar
- 1 teaspoon kosher salt, or more if needed
- 1 teaspoon red pepper flakes
- 3 tablespoons chopped basil leaves

TOPPINGS

- 2 tablespoons extra-virgin olive oil
- ½ pound mushrooms such as cremini, shiitake, chanterelle, oyster, or hen of the woods, tough stems removed, sliced
- ½ teaspoon kosher salt
- 1 or 2 grinds of black pepper
- ½ pound provolone cheese, grated (about 2 cups)
- ½ pound fresh mozzarella cheese, grated (about 2 cups)
- 6 ounces Southern Italian-style spicy dry sausage, such as Napoletano piccante, sliced, or 15 thin slices spicy coppa, stacked and halved to form half moons
- Basil leaves, for garnish

A pizza stone is not optional—there is no better way to achieve a crispy crust in a home oven. Be sure to preheat it aggressively; it takes a solid 30 minutes to get a ceramic slab up to 500°F.

If you want to
use dough from
your favorite
local pizzeria or
even store-bought
dough, you'll need
¾ pound. (Luigi's,
down the block from
our place, sells me
1½-pound blobs for
four bucks—enough
for two medium-plus
pies.) For the sauce,
if you want to sub in
your family's recipe,
use about a cup.

1 Make the dough: In the bowl of a food processor fitted with the steel blade, combine the flour, salt, and yeast, and pulse to blend. Then, with the blade running continuously, add the oil and water, and continue processing until the dough forms a ball and spins around in the bowl, about 30 seconds. Turn the dough out onto a lightly floured surface and knead until smooth, just a minute or two. Then, rub about a tablespoon olive oil into a large bowl, add the dough, and turn to coat with oil. Cover with plastic wrap, and let rise in a warm place until doubled in size, about 2 hours.

2 Make the sauce: Dump the tomatoes and their juices into a food processor and pulse 3 or 4 times to produce a coarse chop.

3 In a medium saucepan, heat the oil over medium heat and cook the shallot until tender, about 6 minutes. Add the garlic and cook until fragrant, 1 minute. Add the tomatoes, vinegar, sugar, salt, and pepper flakes, increase the heat to high, and bring to a boil. Reduce the heat, and simmer until slightly reduced, 20 minutes. (Do not permit a full boil.) Add the basil, taste, and season with salt if needed.

4 When you're ready to bake, put a pizza stone on a rack in the middle of the oven, and preheat the oven to 500°F for a solid 30 minutes—it takes that long to truly bring everything up to temp.

5 Meanwhile, start on the toppings: Place a large skillet over medium-high heat and add the olive oil. When it is just starting to smoke, add the mushrooms, salt, and pepper. Toss to coat, and cook until lightly browned, 5 to 7 minutes. Remove from the heat.

6 On a lightly floured surface, punch down the dough and divide in half. Return half to the bowl, and cover with plastic wrap. Press the other half into a thick, 8-inch disk, and let rest, covered with a damp kitchen towel, for

(recipe continues)

I pick up the cured meats for this pie at the great Di Palo's Fine Foods in New York's Little Italy; if you don't have an Italian market or other gourmet shop nearby, most prosciutto is still a step up from supermarket pepperoni.

15 minutes. Then, roll, pull, stretch, and/or throw the dough with your hands clenched into fists—whatever works for you—until it's about $1/8$ inch thin and the shape you want, either disklike or rectangular.

7 Dust a pizza peel or large cutting board generously and evenly with cornmeal, which adds crunch and allows you to slide the finished pie onto the pizza stone. Transfer the first crust to the peel, and shake the peel to make sure the crust slides around on it.

8 Spoon a scant cup of sauce onto the dough, then arrange half the cheeses, meat, and mushrooms on top. Slide onto the hot stone and bake until the cheese is bubbling and browned, 7 to 10 minutes. Remove to a cutting board, garnish with basil leaves, and let rest for a moment or two. Slice and serve immediately. Repeat with the remaining dough and toppings.

THE PIZZAIOLO'S SECRET: 00 FLOUR

You can make a fine pizza or pasta with all-purpose or bread flour. But it bears pointing out that true, Italian-style pizza is a flatbread with some garnishes on top—that is, it's really about the crust, not 5 pounds of cheese—and that crust deserves to be made with the best ingredients. Ask the guy tossing dough in any serious pizza place, and he'll tell you, spend a few extra bucks for Italian-style 00 (that's "double-zero") flour. You'll never go back.

In Italy, flours are categorized by how finely they're ground: 1, 0, or the talcum-powder texture of 00. Because of that grind and a protein content slightly lower than most all-purpose flours, 00 flour produces an incomparably supple and easy-to-handle dough that won't fight back as you stretch it into shape. Best of all, the flavor is great, and the texture is a perfect combination of crispy outside, tender inside. All-purpose tends to produce crusts that are somewhat chewier.

Double-zero is available at better markets or online; try Antico Molino Caputo Tipo 00 or King Arthur's Italian Style (kingarthurflour.com; hint: King Arthur has flat-rate delivery; go in with like-minded friends and order a bag for each cook).

BETTER-THAN-BEEF **Turkey Burgers** WITH ACTUALLY CRISPY OVEN FRIES MAKES 8 BURGERS

I'M NOT MUCH of a calorie counter, but I still find sensible ways to reduce fat in my cooking. One place it's easy to do that, believe it or not, is burgers. It's not the beefy flavor or fattiness of ground chuck that makes me love hamburgers. It's the texture, the juiciness, the char, the toppings. It's a great bun. I can get all of those things from a well-made turkey burger—and it's appealingly less greasy. My favorite approach uses Asian flavors, a healthy dose of garlic and cayenne, and most important, a whole cup of chopped wild mushrooms, which packs the patties with time-release juiciness bombs. Of course, you can't have burgers without fries. Mine are 1/8-inch-thick chips, roasted with olive oil in a piping-hot oven—and they're fantastic. Salt them while they're hot (the salt sticks better) and serve with fresh refrigerator pickles (page 16).

2 pounds ground turkey

1 cup chopped cremini mushroom caps

½ cup finely chopped red onion

2 garlic cloves, minced

2 teaspoons minced peeled fresh ginger

⅓ cup fresh bread crumbs (made from stale bread)

¼ teaspoon cayenne

1 tablespoon soy sauce

2 teaspoons mirin

2 teaspoons toasted sesame oil

1 large egg

8 burger buns

Condiments, such as mustard, mayonnaise, relish, and pickles, for serving

1 Preheat a grill or grill pan to medium-high.

2 Cut out 8 (5 × 5-inch) squares of wax paper or parchment. Combine the turkey, mushrooms, onion, garlic, ginger, bread crumbs, cayenne, soy, mirin, sesame oil, and egg in a large bowl and mix together with your hands until just combined. Shape into 1-inch-thick patties, placing each burger on a square of wax paper (ground turkey is very sticky, and the paper makes it easier to handle).

3 Grill the burgers, turning once, until charred and cooked through, 5 to 7 minutes per side; use your spatula to feel the burgers as they get firmer from cooking. Let rest for a few minutes off the grill, then serve on the buns with the condiments of your choice.

(recipe continues)

Actually Crispy Oven Fries SERVES 4

1½ pounds russet potatoes (about 3), scrubbed but not peeled

3 tablespoons extra-virgin olive oil

Kosher salt

1 Preheat the oven to 450°F (and if you have a convection oven, turn that feature on).

2 Line 2 baking sheets with parchment paper. In a food processor fitted with a ⅛-inch slicing blade, slice the potatoes. Immediately place in a large bowl and toss thoroughly with the olive oil to prevent them from discoloring. Spread in a single layer on the baking sheets, and bake until the potatoes start browning on the bottom, about 10 minutes.

3 Pull the sheets from oven, noting which one was above the other so that you can swap them. With a spatula, flip the potatoes, making sure to keep them in a single layer. Sprinkle both sheets generously with salt (salt sticks to hot, freshly cooked food), and bake until crisped through and browned, about 10 minutes. Keep an eye on things; thin chips can burn quickly.

4 Transfer the fries to a bowl lined with paper towels or newspaper and serve immediately.

Pork shoulder is one of my favorite cuts of meat, even though at first glance it's ugly, fatty, and tough. If you cook it for a long time, the fat renders, the toughness melts away, and you have a really flavorful roast. It's also cheap—great for feeding a crowd. Here are three different ways to enjoy it, starting with the quintessential slow-and-low barbecue classic, pulled pork, and moving on to Mexican and Indian versions.

NORTH CAROLINA Pulled Pork SERVES ABOUT 12

FOR THIS CAROLINA-STYLE barbecue, the meat is rubbed with dry spices (usually) and cooked slow and low over smoldering charcoal for upward of 8 hours—until the fat and sinew melts down and the meat falls off the bone (or is actually *pulled* off, hence the name). Then, you add a spicy, vinegary sauce, pile the pork high on toasted buns, and serve with pickled red onions. Pork that's cooked this way turns pink from the surface to about half an inch inside, and is covered with fabulously crusty burned bits.

DRY RUB

- 2 tablespoons sweet paprika
- 2 tablespoons packed light brown sugar
- 4 teaspoons kosher salt
- 1½ teaspoons chili powder
- ¼ teaspoon cayenne
- ¼ teaspoon dried oregano
- ¼ teaspoon dried thyme
- ¼ teaspoon ground cumin
- ¼ teaspoon freshly ground black pepper
- ¼ teaspoon garlic powder
- ¼ teaspoon onion powder

PORK

- 1 (5- to 7-pound) bone-in pork shoulder with a good cap of fat
- 12 hamburger buns, toasted
- Vinegar Sauce (recipe follows)
- Pickled Red Onions (recipe follows)

1 Make the dry rub: Combine the paprika, sugar, salt, chili powder, cayenne, oregano, thyme, cumin, pepper, garlic powder, and onion powder.

2 Cook the pork: Fire up your grill, then tighten the upper and lower vents until almost closed to bring the temperature to between 300°F and 325°F (if your grill doesn't have a built-in thermometer, put an instant-read in the upper vent). If using charcoal, be prepared to refuel with hot coals every hour or so.

(recipe continues)

As a shortcut, you can use the grill for only the first couple hours of cooking—more than enough to get smoky flavor—and finish cooking the pork in the oven.

3 Rinse the pork and pat dry with paper towels. Rub all over with the dry rub. Put the pork in a disposable foil pan on the grill. Close the grill, and smoke, monitoring the grill temperature carefully, until the internal temperature of the pork reaches 190°F, 6 to 8 hours. Let cool, and then shred with your fingers, setting aside the bone to cook with beans (Mmm) and discarding the excess fat.

4 In a large pot or Dutch oven with a lid, combine the pulled meat with the Vinegar Sauce. When you're ready to serve, reheat the pork and sauce to a simmer. Use tongs to load up the toasted buns with meat, and serve with the Pickled Red Onions.

Vinegar Sauce MAKES 2 CUPS

1 cup apple cider vinegar

¼ cup ketchup

¼ cup packed light brown sugar

2 teaspoons red pepper flakes

2 teaspoons kosher salt

½ teaspoon cracked black pepper

Stir together the vinegar, ketchup, sugar, pepper flakes, salt, and pepper until the salt and sugar dissolve.

Pickled Red Onions MAKES ABOUT 2 CUPS

½ cup cider or white vinegar

½ cup sugar

1½ teaspoons kosher salt

1 large red onion, halved and thinly sliced

In a small saucepan over high heat, bring the vinegar, sugar, and salt to a boil, then pour over the onion. Cool to room temperature and store in the refrigerator for up to a few weeks. Drain before serving.

PORK AND BLACK BEAN Tinga WITH CHIPOTLE SERVES 4 TO 6

THIS SPICY MEXICAN classic makes for the best tacos you've ever tasted—double or triple the recipe, and you've got the perfect dish for a crowd. Bonus: you end up with a couple extra cups of pork stock, which makes for fantastic soups and beans. Look for raw, Mexican-style chorizo, not the cured, Spanish variety.

4 pounds bone-in pork shoulder (preferable) or 2 pounds boneless

1 large yellow onion, quartered, plus 1 medium yellow onion, chopped

3 garlic cloves, smashed, plus 1 clove, chopped

4 sprigs of thyme

1 tablespoon kosher salt

2 tablespoons extra-virgin olive oil

1 (4-ounce) raw chorizo sausage, diced

1 (28-ounce) can chopped tomatoes

1 bay leaf

1 canned chipotle pepper in adobo sauce, chopped

1 (15-ounce) can black beans, rinsed and drained

1 tablespoon red wine vinegar

12 (6-inch) corn tortillas

1 Hass avocado, diced, tossed with a little lime juice

Sour cream, crumbled queso fresco (fresh, white Mexican cheese), chopped cilantro leaves, and lime wedges, for serving

1 Put the pork in a Dutch oven with the quartered onion, smashed garlic, thyme, and salt and fill with water until the meat is just covered. Bring to a boil, then reduce the heat, and simmer until the meat is fall-off-the-bone tender, 1½ hours.

2 Reserving the cooking liquid, remove the meat to a platter. While the meat is cooling, strain the cooking liquid, remove fat with a fat separator (or spoon it off the top), and pour the stock into a separate saucepan. Bring to a boil over high heat, and reduce for about 15 minutes to make about 3 cups of pork stock. When the pork has cooled enough to handle, discard the fat cap and bones, and shred (I find a combination of 2 forks, or even a potato masher, helpful for this).

3 In the Dutch oven, heat the olive oil over medium-high. Add the chopped onion, chopped garlic, chorizo, and shredded pork, and cook, stirring often, until the meat is browned, about 10 minutes. Add the tomatoes, bay leaf, 1 cup pork stock (refrigerate or freeze the rest for another use), chipotle, the beans, and vinegar, and bring to a boil. Reduce heat, and simmer until most liquid has evaporated, about 20 minutes. Remove bay leaf.

4 Warm the tortillas in moistened paper towels in the microwave oven for 30 seconds, or for a few seconds in a dry skillet on high heat, and serve with the pork, avocado, sour cream, queso fresco, cilantro, and lime wedges.

Pork Vindaloo WITH PEAS AND CAULIFLOWER SERVES 4

I TAKE A SIMPLIFIED approach to this vivid and (usually) fiery Indian stew, adapting a recipe by my friend Suvir Saran, the brilliant Indian chef. Because it's so easy and so attractive, I've taken the rather extreme liberty of adding vegetables, making a one-pot meal; note that the cauliflower turns a beautiful golden color from the turmeric. Serve with basmati rice.

1½ teaspoons cumin seeds

1½ teaspoons coriander seeds

8 cardamom pods

2 teaspoons red pepper flakes

⅛ teaspoon ground cinnamon

¼ teaspoon ground cloves

1 teaspoon ground turmeric

6 garlic cloves, chopped

1 (2-inch) piece fresh ginger, peeled and minced

2 tablespoons white vinegar

Juice of ½ lemon

Kosher salt and freshly ground black pepper

2 pounds boneless pork shoulder, skin and excess fat trimmed, cut into 4 large chunks

1 (14.5-ounce) can whole peeled tomatoes, drained

2 medium yellow onions, quartered

3 tablespoons vegetable oil

1 (10-ounce) bag frozen peas

8 ounces cauliflower florets

1 Grind the cumin, coriander, cardamom, and red pepper flakes in a spice grinder or mortar and pestle. In a small bowl, combine with the cinnamon, cloves, turmeric, garlic, ginger, vinegar, lemon juice, and 2 teaspoons salt to make a paste. Smear the paste all over the pork, cover with plastic wrap, and refrigerate for at least 2 and up to 4 hours.

2 Puree the tomatoes and onions in a food processor.

3 In a Dutch oven or heavy casserole over medium-high, heat the oil. Add the meat and sear on all sides, about 10 minutes. Add the tomato mixture, ½ teaspoon salt, and water to almost cover the meat (about 1 cup), and bring to a boil. Reduce the heat, and simmer, covered, for 1 hour.

4 Add the peas and cauliflower, season to taste with salt and pepper, and simmer until the meat is fall-off-the-bone tender, 15 minutes or so. On a cutting board, shred the meat with 2 forks, return it to the pot, warm through, and serve.

FAT TEDDY'S Baby-Back Ribs SERVES 4

DON'T LAUGH—packing on pounds is a fairly unsurprising occupational hazard in my business. Still, there are few things I'd rather barbecue than baby backs. I love the chewiness, the burned bits, the primal act of gnawing pork off a bone. I use a ceramic-lined charcoal cooker similar to the Big Green Egg, because it makes it easy to regulate the temperature, but you can do this in a barbecue kettle, too (you might have to replenish charcoal, though) or in a gas grill or oven. This is indirect cooking; that is, not directly over the coals. Push coals to opposite sides of the grill, and put a foil drip tray between. If you plan on cooking lots of ribs, a rack that holds them upright is a good investment.

2 racks baby-back pork ribs

Dry Rub (page 189)

2 cups apple cider

Bourbon-Bacon Barbecue Sauce with Chipotle (recipe follows) or other good-quality barbecue sauce

If you like, put some cider in a clean spray bottle, and spritz the ribs a few times as they smoke.

For store-bought barbecue sauce, I like Bone Suckin' Sauce, which is the right thickness and is natural.

1 First, you need to remove the silvery membrane from the back side of the ribs, or your marinade won't get to the meat. Using a paring knife to scrape the membrane from the bone at the small end of the rack, loosen enough that you can grab it, using a paper towel for grip. With practice, you should be able to pull the entire membrane off in one go.

2 Rinse the pork, and pat dry with paper towels. Cover both sides of the racks completely with the dry rub, rubbing it into the meat. Wrap tightly with plastic wrap and marinate for at least 4 hours and preferably overnight.

3 Preheat a grill to 325°F. Soak 1 cup applewood, hickory, or mesquite wood chips in water (or additional apple cider) for 1 hour.

4 When your grill is ready, drain the wood chips and throw them on the coals. Put the ribs in a disposable foil pan on the rack, close the grill lid, and smoke them for 1 hour.

5 Remove the pan from the grill, and let cool for a few minutes. Add the apple cider to the pan, and cover tightly with foil. Continue smoking until the meat has shrunk back from the bones and is falling-off tender, or to taste, 30 minutes to 1 hour.

6 Remove the foil, brush both sides of the ribs with barbecue sauce, and cook, uncovered, for 10 minutes more. Carve into easy-handling racks of 3 or 4 ribs each. Serve with extra sauce.

Bourbon-Bacon Barbecue Sauce with Chipotle

MAKES ABOUT 2 CUPS

IT JUST AIN'T RIGHT: You spend big money on ribs, nurture them over hot coals all afternoon until they're perfectly, fall-off-the-bone tender, and then you drench them with high-fructose corn syrup, artificial flavors, and preservatives? Of course not! I love this recipe for its tempered sweetness, the hint of bacon (which is optional), and the smoky kick of chipotle peppers. This is great on pork, chicken, brisket—you name it.

2 slices bacon, diced, or 2 tablespoons extra-virgin olive oil

1 tablespoon extra-virgin olive oil

1 medium red onion, diced

1 tablespoon minced garlic

1 tablespoon minced peeled fresh ginger

1 medium tomato, diced

2 tablespoons chopped canned chipotle peppers in adobo

½ cup orange juice

Juice of 1 lime

½ cup apple cider vinegar

⅓ cup ketchup

¼ to ½ cup bourbon, to taste

2 tablespoons honey

½ teaspoon kosher salt

¼ teaspoon freshly ground black pepper

½ cup chopped cilantro leaves

Remember to brush on wet sauces only during the last 10 minutes of cooking; add them too soon, and the sugars in the sauce will take the fatal turn past caramelized to burned.

1 In a medium saucepan over medium-low heat, sauté the bacon (if using) until crispy, about 8 minutes. Remove with a slotted spoon to drain on paper towels, reserving the drippings in the pan. Add the olive oil and onion, and cook until soft, about 7 minutes. Add the garlic and ginger, and cook until fragrant, 1 minute. Dump in the tomato, chipotle, orange juice, lime juice, vinegar, ketchup, bourbon, honey, salt, and pepper, bring to a boil, reduce the heat, and simmer until slightly thickened, 20 minutes.

2 Remove from the heat, let cool, and stir in the cilantro. Refrigerate and use within a week or two, or freeze for longer storage.

THE BUTCHER'S BACK!

Somehow, suddenly, we have butchers again. After decades of having to settle for only the cuts that giant meat corporations want to sell us, factory-farmed and shrink-wrapped in Upton Sinclair horror shows somewhere out west, now comes a new generation of devoted meat experts: young, tattooed, and passionate about ordering heritage breed critters whole, and breaking them down the old-fashioned way. This is true, at least, in Brooklyn, where there are enough interested consumers to support these gourmet purveyors. This kind of meat is more expensive (on the surface) than the mass-produced kind, but it permits the dedicated cook to support small farms and small farmers who produce more flavorful and interesting breeds of pork, beef, duck, and lamb, and is particularly great for those of us who want organic, humanely raised, and/or grass-fed animals. It's also great when you want an unusual cut, or

a particularly delicious pork chop for a special occasion. Or, in our case, when you want to shoot the breeze with like-minded food dorks—our local kitchen shop and butcher, The Brooklyn Kitchen/The Meat Hook (right, home to butcher Ben Turley), has become the kind of hangout that record stores used to be in the seventies. They make charcuterie, *kombucha,* and vinegar; they sell Brooklyn-made pickles and ricotta; and they offer an extensive program of cooking classes (www .thebrooklynkitchen.com). Please support your local, independent butcher!

Rack of Pork WITH PEAR-APPLE COMPOTE SERVES 4

THE STANDING RIB ROAST is the iconic fancy entrée, especially around the holidays, with or without the little white hats on the bones. If you can find yourself a butcher and give him a few days' notice, this special-occasion cut need not come from a cow: brined nicely and roasted until just still pink, a rack of pork is a great thing to cook and eat, standing or otherwise. It's really just a row of bone-in pork chops that haven't been separated, with the fat scraped off the ribs (the term is "frenched") to make them prettier. I buy mine from the lovely and talented Brent Young at The Meat Hook, in Brooklyn, one of the new breed of butchers in my town (see page 197). And I'm not kidding: he had the little white hats, and he threw them in, no charge. And then I forgot to put them on.

PORK

1 cup kosher salt

½ cup honey

2 garlic cloves, smashed

2 (6-inch) sprigs rosemary

1 bay leaf

10 juniper berries

10 black peppercorns

1 (2-pound) pork loin roast with 4 rib bones, trimmed and frenched

1 tablespoon extra-virgin olive oil

PEAR-APPLE COMPOTE

1 shallot, chopped

1 Granny Smith apple, peeled, cored, and diced

1 Bosc pear, peeled, cored, and diced

½ cup dried cranberries

½ cup orange juice

½ cup apple cider

1 tablespoon packed light brown sugar

1 tablespoon Dijon mustard

2 teaspoons chopped rosemary leaves

½ teaspoon kosher salt

¼ teaspoon freshly ground black pepper

⅛ teaspoon cayenne

Give yourself a day before serving in order to brine the roast overnight—it makes all the difference in flavor and juiciness.

1 Brine the pork: In a small saucepan over high heat, dissolve the salt and honey in 1 cup water. Remove from the heat, add the garlic, rosemary, bay leaf, juniper, and peppercorns, and steep until the water cools to room temperature, about 20 minutes. Pour into a large food-storage container with a lid, and add very cold water until you have a gallon. Submerge the pork in the brine and marinate in the refrigerator overnight.

2 To roast the pork, preheat the oven to 350°F.

3 Rinse the pork and pat dry (discard the brine). Heat an ovenproof sauté pan over medium-high heat for a few minutes, add the oil, and sear the roast well on all sides to a deep golden brown, about 10 minutes. Put the pork in the oven and roast until the center reaches 150°F for medium-well, about 40 minutes. Remove to a cutting board, tent with foil, and let rest for 15 minutes. The temperature will rise to about 155°F.

4 While the meat is resting, make the compote: Drain all but 2 tablespoons fat from the roasting pan. Put the pan over 2 burners on medium heat, and sauté the shallot for 5 minutes. Add the apple, pear, cranberries, orange juice, cider, brown sugar, mustard, rosemary, salt, pepper, and cayenne; bring to a boil; reduce the heat to medium; and simmer until the fruit is soft and the sauce is thickened, 5 to 8 minutes.

5 Carve the pork into individual chops and serve with the compote.

MEXICAN Leg of Lamb BARBACOA

SERVES 6 WITH LEFTOVERS FOR SAMMIES

LEG OF LAMB has always made me think of fancy, afternoon Easter suppers on silver platters, followed by great cold sandwiches for days. It did not, until recently, make me think of Mexican food. But slather this tender and sturdily flavored roast in a paste of vinegar, ground anchos and guajillos, great gobs of garlic, and a complex blend of sweet and savory spices, and you'll be transported to someone's madre's house in the Yucàtan countryside. This is a real center-of-the-table showstopper.

1 (4- to 4½-pound)
  boneless leg of lamb

4 dried guajillo chiles,
  stemmed, seeded, and
  torn into a few pieces

4 dried ancho chiles,
  stemmed, seeded, and
  torn into a few pieces

¼ cup thyme leaves (from
  about 12 sprigs)

1 head garlic, peeled and
  chopped

1 cup chopped yellow onion

⅓ cup cider vinegar

3 tablespoons dried oregano

2 teaspoons ground cumin

½ teaspoon ground
  cinnamon

¼ teaspoon ground cloves

¼ teaspoon ground allspice

2 tablespoons kosher salt

1 tablespoon sugar

Depending on how the lamb was cut, you may want—post-marinating—to fold it onto itself and tie it with cotton string; I like it to be about an even, 5-inch barrel shape, which I find cooks most evenly and looks best on the table after roasting.

1 Put the lamb in a large, nonreactive container.

2 Put the guajillo and ancho chiles in a bowl, cover with hot tap water, and let stand for 15 minutes to soften.

3 Put the thyme, garlic, onion, cider vinegar, oregano, cumin, cinnamon, cloves, allspice, salt, and sugar in a blender. Drain the chiles, reserving the soaking water, and add them to the blender. Measure ½ cup of the soaking water, and pour it into the blender. Blend to a smooth paste, adding more soaking water if needed.

4 Rub the chile mixture all over the lamb, cover, and marinate in the refrigerator for at least 4 hours, or, better yet, overnight.

5 Preheat the oven to 325°F.

6 Put the lamb directly in a roasting pan, without a rack. Pour all of the chile mixture over and around the lamb. Cover the roasting pan with foil, and place in the oven. Roast the lamb for 3 to 3½ hours, until the meat is very tender.

7 Let rest for 15 minutes, then remove any string, slice, and serve with the sauce from the pan poured over the top.

Savory Bread Pudding WITH RED ONION AND SPINACH SERVES 6 TO 8

BREAD PUDDING USUALLY means dessert, but it's also a great format for savory flavors—in this case, a satisfying vegetarian main dish that fills your home with the aroma of Gruyère as it bakes. It's also tailor-made for preparing up to a day ahead.

4 large eggs

1½ teaspoons Dijon mustard

1½ teaspoons kosher salt

A few grinds of black pepper

⅛ teaspoon cayenne

1½ teaspoons thyme leaves

2½ cups whole milk

8 ounces Gruyère, grated (about 2 cups)

1 stale baguette or 1-pound loaf crusty bread, hard ends removed, crusts left on, cut into 1-inch cubes (about 8 cups)

2 pounds spinach, tough stems removed

2 tablespoons extra-virgin olive oil, plus more for the dish

1 large red onion, chopped

2 garlic cloves, chopped

1 In a medium bowl, lightly beat together the eggs, mustard, salt, pepper, cayenne, and thyme. Whisk in the milk and Gruyère. Put the bread cubes in a large bowl, pour the egg mixture over the bread, and toss. Give the bread 15 to 30 minutes to absorb the mixture, especially if the bread was very stale and hard, tossing occasionally.

2 Bring a large pot of water to a boil over high heat, and season well with salt. Prepare a large bowl of ice water, and place a colander in the sink. Blanch the spinach in the boiling water for 90 seconds (it will shrink—a lot). Drain in the colander, and then immediately submerge the colander into the ice water to stop the cooking. Allow the spinach to cool for several minutes; then squeeze as much liquid from the spinach as you can, putting the spinach back into the colander.

3 Preheat the oven to 375°F. Grease a 9 × 13-inch baking dish with olive oil.

4 Heat the olive oil in a sauté pan over medium heat. Add the onion and cook until soft, about 8 minutes. Add the garlic and cook until fragrant, 1 minute. Remove from the heat.

5 Stir the spinach and onion into the bread mixture. Pour into the prepared dish, pressing down with a spatula. Bake until bubbling and browned, about 45 minutes.

If your bread is fresh instead of stale, cut it up, and then dry it on a sheet pan in a 350°F oven for 15 minutes.

SERVES 8 TO 10

I LOVE AN ANTIPASTO platter for its variety, color, and vivid flavor. And as great as artisanal salumi and cheeses are, the vegetables traditional to this platter bring a lot to the party, too. Here, the flavors and textures of those veggies are celebrated with a whole new treatment: layered in a hollowed-out loaf of whole-grain bread, sweetened with a touch of balsamic vinegar and roasted garlic, and then pressed—it's like a vegetable terrine on a bun. You can cook this indoors or out, and it's gorgeous on a buffet. Feel free to swap other vegetables in or out, except the caramelized onions, which are a must.

1 loaf country bread, about 4 inches wide and 12 inches long

1 head of garlic

2 tablespoons plus 1 teaspoon extra-virgin olive oil, plus more for drizzling

1 zucchini, sliced ¼ inch thick on the diagonal

1 yellow summer squash, sliced ¼ inch thick on the diagonal

1 small eggplant, peeled and sliced ¼ inch thick

1 red onion, cut into ½-inch wedges

Kosher salt and freshly ground black pepper

1 jarred roasted red bell pepper, cut into 1-inch-wide strips

¼ cup basil leaves, thinly sliced

1 tablespoon balsamic vinegar

½ cup pickled peperoncini peppers, drained and coarsely chopped

½ cup pitted kalamata olives, chopped

1. Preheat the oven to 400°F or heat a grill to medium-high.

2. Slice off the top third of the loaf and set aside. Scoop out the inside of the rest of the loaf, reserving the bread for another use such as croutons, and leaving about ½ inch all around the loaf.

3. Cut the tip off the head of garlic, cutting through the top of the cloves, and put the head on a piece of foil. Drizzle 1 teaspoon of the olive oil into the head of garlic, and wrap in the foil. Roast until soft, 15 minutes on the grill or 30 to 35 minutes in the oven. Remove the garlic from the foil and cool; then, squeeze the cloves from their skins into a small bowl.

4. Increase the oven temperature to 450°F. In separate pans, drizzle the zucchini, summer squash, eggplant, and onion with olive oil and then toss. Roast until all are charred and softened, about 20 minutes; keep each vegetable separate. Season each vegetable lightly with salt and pepper.

5. Put the roasted pepper in a bowl with the basil, the remaining 2 tablespoons olive oil, and the balsamic, and toss to coat.

6. Put the hollowed-out bread on the grill or in the oven to toast for a few minutes, until lightly crusty. Spread the inside with the roasted garlic, then layer into the bread, the zucchini, summer squash, eggplant, onion, peperoncini, roasted pepper, and olives. Replace the top, wrap tightly with plastic wrap, and refrigerate, placing a cast-iron skillet or something else heavy on top to press it down, for at least 2 hours or overnight. Unwrap, slice, and serve.

Desserts

butterscotch pots de crème with scotched pecans 209

CHOCOLATE–SOUR CREAM LAYER CAKE WITH CREAM-CHEESE FROSTING AND HAZELNUTS 211

elderflower sabayon with seasonal berries 215

DARK CHOCOLATE SANDWICH COOKIES WITH MASCARPONE FILLING 216

vanilla ice cream with honey 221

SALTED CARAMEL ICE CREAM 224

butter pecan brittle 228

CHILE-SPICED HOT FUDGE SAUCE 229

Butterscotch Pots de Crème WITH
SCOTCHED PECANS SERVES 8

FIRST, A PROMISE: Your guests will in*hale* this custard. They will scrape the bottoms of their ramekins with spoons, fingers, tongues, whatever it takes. They will probably also moan and refer to deities. Just so you know.

Meanwhile, there's been a lot of talk lately about commingling the sweet and savory (you know, black pepper ice cream, bacon toffee, and so on). Well, as this luscious concoction shows, those worlds have never been completely separate. Salt, which is a crucial (but background) ingredient in virtually every savory *and* sweet dish, plays an important role in this one. Butterscotch, which as you might imagine is made with butter and Scotch whiskey, also leans heavily on salt for its unique and unbeatable flavor. I especially love this dessert because it transports me immediately back in time to my grandfather's candy dish.

POTS DE CRÈME

- 3 cups heavy cream
- 3 (2-inch) strips lemon zest
- 1 vanilla bean, split lengthwise and scraped
- ¾ teaspoon table salt
- ½ teaspoon ground cardamom
- 6 tablespoons unsalted butter
- 1 cup packed dark brown sugar
- 3 tablespoons Scotch whiskey
- 6 large egg yolks

PECANS

- 1 cup pecans
- 2 tablespoons Scotch whiskey
- 1 tablespoon unsalted butter
- 1 teaspoon granulated sugar
- 1 teaspoon table salt

Lightly sweetened whipped cream, for serving (optional)

1 Make the pots de crème: Preheat the oven to 300°F.

2 Put the heavy cream, lemon zest, vanilla bean and seeds, salt, and cardamom in a saucepan over medium heat. Bring just to a boil, remove pan from the heat, and set aside to steep.

(recipe continues)

3   In another saucepan, heat the butter and brown sugar over medium heat until the mixture starts to bubble. Stir in the Scotch, and cook until the whiskey has evaporated, about 1 minute.

4   Put the egg yolks in a mixing bowl and add a little bit of the butter and brown sugar mixture, whisking to temper the yolks. Add more, bit by bit, and whisk until it has all been incorporated. Strain the cream mixture into the bowl and whisk to combine.

5   Put 8 (4-ounce) ramekins in a large roasting pan, leaving space between them. Fill the ramekins all the way up with the cream mixture. Pour hot tap water into the roasting pan to come halfway up the ramekins. Cover with foil and place in the oven. Bake for 20 minutes, then remove the foil, and bake until they are just set, about 35 minutes.

6   While the pots de crème are in the oven, make the pecans: Put an ovenproof skillet over medium-high heat and add the pecans, Scotch, butter, granulated sugar, and salt, and cook until the Scotch has evaporated. Transfer the pan to the oven and roast the pecans until deep golden, 15 minutes. Remove from the oven, and let cool.

7   Carefully remove the pots de crème from the oven—watch for sloshing, as that water is obviously very hot—and let them cool in the roasting pan for at least 40 minutes. When the pots de crème are cool, wrap each one in plastic wrap and chill until ready to serve.

8   To serve, place a dollop of lightly sweetened whipped cream on each pot, if desired, or just top each with 2 or 3 pecans.

Chocolate–Sour Cream Layer Cake

WITH CREAM-CHEESE FROSTING AND HAZELNUTS

MAKES 1 (9-INCH) LAYER CAKE; SERVES 8 TO 10

THERE IS A LOT of chocolate in this cake, and that flavor is definitely the star. But what makes this Barry's best chocolate cake yet is, of all things, the tangy richness from both the sour cream in the batter and the cream cheese in the frosting. A hint of espresso lends still more complexity. And nothing tastes better with chocolate than hazelnuts, whose wonderful, toasty flavor is bolstered with a shot of Italian hazelnut liqueur in the frosting.

CAKE

- 1 cup (2 sticks) unsalted butter, at room temperature, plus more for the pans
- 1½ cups all-purpose flour, plus more for the pan
- ¾ cup unsweetened cocoa powder (not Dutch processed)
- 2 tablespoons instant coffee or espresso flakes
- 2 teaspoons baking powder
- ¾ teaspoon baking soda
- ¾ teaspoon table salt
- 1 cup sour cream
- ⅓ cup whole milk
- 1 tablespoon pure vanilla extract
- 1½ cups packed light brown sugar
- 3 large eggs, at room temperature

FROSTING

- 1 cup hazelnuts
- 1 cup (2 sticks) unsalted butter, at room temperature
- 1 (8-ounce) package cream cheese, at room temperature
- 5 ounces unsweetened chocolate, melted and cooled
- 2 tablespoons Frangelico hazelnut liqueur
- 3½ cups confectioners' sugar

1 Make the cake: Put a rack in the center of the oven and preheat the oven to 350°F. Butter and flour two 9-inch round cake pans.

2 In a large bowl, whisk together the flour, cocoa powder, instant coffee, baking powder, baking soda, and salt.

3 In a medium bowl, whisk together the sour cream, milk, and vanilla, and allow to come to room temperature.

(recipe continues)

4 In a stand mixer with the paddle attachment on medium-high speed, beat the butter and brown sugar until fluffy. Reduce the speed to medium-low and add the eggs, one at a time, mixing thoroughly for a minute or two after each egg. Scrape down the bowl with a spatula.

5 On medium-low speed, add one-third of the flour mixture, and then half of the milk mixture. Repeat, mixing thoroughly for a minute or two after each addition, and scraping down the bowl regularly; end with the final third of the flour.

6 Divide the batter evenly between the pans. Bake until a toothpick or wooden skewer inserted into the centers comes out clean, 25 to 30 minutes. Do not jostle or test the cakes until they have baked for a full 25 minutes, or you may cause them to fall. Cool the cakes for 5 minutes on a rack, then remove them from the pans, and cool completely on the rack. Keep the oven on.

7 Make the frosting: Toast the hazelnuts on a baking sheet in the oven until fragrant, 5 to 8 minutes, watching them carefully to make sure they don't burn. Allow to cool slightly, then roll in a textured clean dish towel to remove most of the skins. Chop coarsely and set aside.

8 Using a stand mixer with the paddle attachment, beat together the butter and cream cheese until fluffy, 3 minutes. Add the chocolate and Frangelico, and mix thoroughly. Gradually beat in the confectioners' sugar until thoroughly combined and fluffy.

9 Assemble the cake: Place one layer top side up on a cake plate. Spread one-third of the frosting over it. Top with the second layer, and frost the top and sides with the remaining frosting. Carefully sprinkle the hazelnuts over the top of the cake, leaving the sides just frosted.

Elderflower Sabayon WITH
SEASONAL BERRIES SERVES 4 TO 6

FOR CENTURIES, COOKING has relied upon ingredients and techniques that convert liquids into gels, gels into solids, and so on (which, to me, makes the controversy about molecular gastronomy seem silly, but anyway . . .). And it would be hard to argue that any ingredient is as magical and versatile in this department as the chicken egg. Here, in an excellent example, egg yolks get whipped into fluffy, ethereal beauty over a double boiler to make a simple, perfect topping for fruit or cake—thicker than a sauce, softer than whipped cream. Instead of the traditional Marsala wine, Barry's modern interpretation uses St. Germain, the heavenly French elderflower liqueur, which pairs beautifully with mixed berries.

4 large egg yolks

¼ cup sugar

⅓ cup St. Germain elderflower liqueur

1 teaspoon fresh lemon juice

½ cup heavy cream

2 pounds mixed fresh berries, such as blackberries, raspberries, blueberries, and sliced strawberries

Sabayon doesn't traditionally call for whipped cream, but folding in a generous dollop results in an extremely soft, creamy sauce.

1 Bring 2 inches of water to a gentle simmer in a large saucepan.

2 Whisk together the egg yolks, sugar, St. Germain, and lemon juice in a large, heatproof mixing bowl. Set the bowl on the pan of simmering water, being careful not to let the bowl touch the water, and whisk the egg mixture until it thickens to the consistency of lightly whipped cream, 5 to 8 minutes. Be careful to scrape the sides of the bowl frequently, or you'll end up with bits of scrambled egg here and there.

3 Remove the bowl from the heat and set it into a larger bowl filled with ice and water. Whisk the mixture occasionally as it cools.

4 In a medium bowl, whip the heavy cream until soft peaks form. Fold the whipped cream into the cooled egg mixture until just combined. Cover and refrigerate until cold, at least 1 hour or up to 5 hours.

5 Divide the berries among 4 small bowls or parfait glasses. Spoon the sabayon over the berries and serve.

Dark Chocolate Sandwich Cookies

WITH MASCARPONE FILLING   MAKES ABOUT 20 SANDWICH COOKIES

BARRY IS RARELY content with one simple element in his desserts. Working on this recipe to cap an Italian menu, it was not enough just to serve deeply decadent, dark-chocolate cookies. Inspired by cannoli, he decided upon a sandwich cookie filled with ricotta and sweet, soft Italian mascarpone cheese, vanilla, and roasted pistachios.

COOKIES

1 cup (2 sticks) unsalted butter, at room temperature

⅔ cup granulated sugar

½ cup packed light brown sugar

3 tablespoons whole milk

½ teaspoon pure vanilla extract

1½ cups all-purpose flour

¾ cup unsweetened cocoa powder (not Dutch processed)

½ teaspoon table salt

¼ teaspoon baking soda

½ cup semisweet chocolate chips, optional

FILLING

1½ cups chopped, roasted, shelled, unsalted pistachios

1½ cups confectioners' sugar

1½ cups mascarpone cheese

¾ cup ricotta

½ teaspoon pure vanilla extract

¾ teaspoon table salt

These cookies are best assembled as close to serving time as possible, or else they lose their crispness.

(recipe continues)

1 Make the cookies: In a stand mixer with the paddle attachment, beat the butter, granulated sugar, and brown sugar until creamy. Mix in the milk and vanilla.

2 In a medium bowl, thoroughly combine the flour, cocoa, salt, and baking soda. Slowly add to the butter mixture while beating on a low speed. Add chocolate chips, if using, and mix until just combined. When evenly mixed, shape the dough into a log about 2 inches thick and roll it in wax paper. Chill in the refrigerator for at least 2 hours or overnight.

3 Preheat the oven to 350°F.

4 Use a sharp knife to slice the cookies into $\frac{1}{3}$-inch-thick disks. Don't worry if cookies break apart as you cut them—pieces can be stuck back together and will bake fine. Arrange 2 inches apart on baking sheets lined with parchment paper. Bake until set, 10 minutes. Cool for a few minutes on the baking sheets, and then remove to racks to cool completely.

5 Make the filling: Set aside half of the chopped pistachios for garnish. Mix the remaining pistachios with the confectioners' sugar, mascarpone cheese, ricotta, vanilla, and salt until just blended; do not overbeat, as the mascarpone will get too thick. Cover and refrigerate until needed.

6 To assemble, put a scoop of filling on the bottom side of a cookie and top with the bottom side of another cookie, so that there is about $\frac{1}{4}$ inch of filling in each sandwich. Coat the filling edges with the reserved pistachios.

My primary weaknesses: salty potato chips, American pale ale, and cheese. Barry's, definitely, is ice cream. There is almost never a cake, a pie, or a tart that he doesn't believe is immeasurably improved with a scoop (or two, or three . . .). Here, he gets right to the point with four rich, custardy flavors—and yummy toppings.

Vanilla Ice Cream WITH HONEY MAKES 1 GENEROUS QUART

OF ALL THE WAYS to flavor frozen cream, there is nothing more elegant or more versatile than vanilla. For a subtle but noticeable twist, Barry sweetens our batches with the light, floral, slightly minty honey from his beehive on our roof in Brooklyn. This recipe can serve as a base for many variations—two of our favorites follow. Or you can try in-season fruits or even subtle spice combinations.

3 cups heavy cream

1 cup whole milk

½ cup honey

2 vanilla beans, split lengthwise and scraped

4 large egg yolks

1 tablespoon pure vanilla extract

The best ice cream is made from the best ingredients: local, low-pasteurized, nonhomogenized milk and cream, and—for vanilla— a double dose of flavoring, straight from the bean itself and also via high-quality extract.

1 Heat the cream, milk, honey, and vanilla beans and seeds in a heavy saucepan over medium heat until hot, being careful not to let the mixture boil and curdle.

2 Lightly whisk the egg yolks in a medium heatproof bowl, then slowly drizzle 1 cup of the hot cream mixture into the yolks while whisking. Pour the yolk mixture into the saucepan of cream; heat, stirring constantly, until the custard thickens slightly and coats the back of a wooden spoon, again being careful not to let it boil and curdle.

3 Pour through a fine-mesh strainer to remove the vanilla beans and any bits of cooked egg yolk. Stir in the vanilla extract. Cover the custard with plastic wrap and refrigerate until cold, about 6 hours. You can speed this process dramatically by partially submerging the bowl of custard in a larger bowl of ice water to form an ice bath, and stirring the custard occasionally until cold. The colder the custard is, the faster the machine will be able to freeze it for ice cream.

4 Follow the directions on your ice cream maker to freeze. Once the mixture is frozen, put it into containers and allow it to "ripen" for at least 2 hours in the freezer.

BARRY'S BROOKLYN BEES

A couple of years ago, having decided against building a chicken coop in our backyard (chickens tend to poop up the joint), Barry and our friend Amy Azzarito thought they could quench their urban-farming imperatives with something simpler: a beehive on the roof of our brownstone. It was certainly fine with me, but I wasn't especially interested in having vast amounts of honey. And then, something happened: we discovered that beekeeping was fascinating and rewarding to us. Watching the ladies build a hive-full of perfect honeycomb, seeing the queen grow the colony at a rate of some thousand eggs a day, knowing that they were foraging as far away as three miles to find nectar, it all got us hopelessly hooked. Best of all, when Barry harvested, we discovered that his bees produced an incredibly light, delicate, floral honey with a faintly minty finish—in short, the best honey we had ever tasted. Which is a good thing, since his hive produces well north of one hundred pounds of the golden stuff

every summer; now we cook with it all the time (and, if you're nice to us, we give it to you). Some people believe that eating honey made from the plants that flower in your neighborhood makes you less susceptible to allergies. I don't know if that's true, but it seems logical-ish. Regardless, raising bees is nothing but good for local flora and for the mysteriously shrinking bee population, generally, and they're really not interested in stinging people unless you're messing with their hive. So don't, and you'll be fine.

If you're intrigued, see if anybody offers beekeeping classes in your area; Barry and Amy learned the craft via the New York City Beekeepers Association, www.nyc-bees.org. And as we like to say, save the bees!

CHOCOLATE ICE CREAM MAKES 1 GENEROUS QUART

Again, the better the chocolate, the better the chocolate ice cream. Try E. Guittard or Valrhona.

Prepare the base for Vanilla Ice Cream with Honey (page 221), omitting the vanilla extract, and stirring in 6 ounces melted high-quality bittersweet chocolate and a pinch of salt before chilling and freezing.

MASCARPONE–SOUR CHERRY ICE CREAM MAKES ABOUT 1½ QUARTS

Here, bright, tart cherries meet sweet, creamy mascarpone cheese to make a balanced and decadent ice cream. It's wonderful on its own or with a generous drizzle of chocolate sauce. You can substitute 1 cup dried tart cherries for the fresh or frozen ones. If you do, the cherries will be a bit firmer once simmered and plumped in the cherry brandy, and the ice cream will be a little less pink without the juice that fresh cherries release when simmered. Either way, delicious.

1 Prepare the base for Vanilla Ice Cream with Honey (page 221), stirring in a pinch of salt before chilling.

2 In a small saucepan over low heat, simmer 12 ounces pitted sour cherries (frozen or fresh) with ¼ cup Kirschwasser cherry brandy until the liquid is slightly thickened and syrupy, about 20 minutes. Cover with plastic wrap, and refrigerate until cold, about 2 hours.

3 Whisk 1 cup mascarpone into the ice cream base until thoroughly combined. Stir in the cold cherry mixture. Follow the directions on your ice cream maker to freeze. Once the mixture is frozen, put it into containers and allow it to "ripen" for at least 2 hours in the freezer.

SALTED CARAMEL Ice Cream MAKES 1 GENEROUS QUART

THIS IS A TWO-SAUCEPAN ice cream—you have to make a traditional ice cream base and a separate caramel recipe—and as such is a bit fussier than most ice cream recipes. But the results are amazing; it's the best ice cream on Earth. The coarse, flaky sea salt incorporates gradually, and with any luck, you'll occasionally bite into an undissolved flake. Barry's favorite to use is a vanilla-infused sea salt by Halen Môn. Because the caramel is fully incorporated into the base, the ice cream stays soft and easily scoopable, with an almost chewy texture.

SALTY CARAMEL

1 cup sugar

1 cup heavy cream

2 teaspoons pure vanilla extract

½ teaspoon flaky sea salt

ICE CREAM BASE

2 cups heavy cream

1 cup whole milk

¼ cup sugar

4 large egg yolks

1 Make the caramel: Put the sugar and ½ cup water in a heavy saucepan over low heat. Cook, stirring, until the sugar is dissolved (the liquid will turn clear), 1 to 2 minutes. Turn the heat up to medium and cook, swirling the pan occasionally for even cooking, until the sugar syrup turns a caramel color, about 20 minutes. When the syrup has turned dark amber, remove it from the heat, and carefully pour in the cream. Stand back, as the caramel will sputter. Continue to stir, and return to low heat if necessary to melt the caramel. Once smooth, remove the caramel from the heat, and stir in the vanilla and salt.

2 Make the ice cream base: Heat the cream, milk, and sugar in a heavy saucepan over medium heat, stirring frequently, until hot, being careful not to let it boil and curdle.

3 Lightly whisk the egg yolks in a medium heatproof bowl, then slowly drizzle 1 cup of the hot cream mixture into the yolks while whisking. Pour the yolk mixture into the saucepan of cream and cook, stirring constantly, until the custard thickens slightly and coats the back of a wooden spoon, again being careful not to let it boil and curdle.

4 Pour through a fine-mesh strainer to remove any bits of cooked egg yolk. Stir in the warm caramel. Cover in plastic wrap and refrigerate until cold, about 6 hours. You can speed this process dramatically by partially

submerging the bowl of custard in a larger bowl of ice water, and stirring the custard occasionally until cold. The colder the custard is, the faster the machine will be able to freeze it for ice cream.

5 Follow the directions on your ice cream maker to freeze. Once the mixture is frozen, put it into containers and allow it to "ripen" for at least 2 hours in the freezer.

BUTTER PECAN **Brittle** MAKES ABOUT 2 POUNDS

GOLDEN-BROWN, GLISTENING brittle with the sweet taste of pecans—this is great broken into a candy dish and served on its own, and better still on top of ice cream.

4 tablespoons (½ stick) unsalted butter, plus more for the baking sheets

3 cups pecans

2 cups sugar

1 cup light corn syrup

2 teaspoons baking soda

1 tablespoon pure vanilla extract

¾ teaspoon flaky sea salt

1 Position a rack in the center of the oven and preheat the oven to 350°F. Butter three baking sheets, and set aside.

2 Spread the pecans on another baking sheet and, stirring occasionally, toast until fragrant, 5 to 7 minutes.

3 Combine the sugar, corn syrup, and ½ cup water in a large saucepan over medium heat, stirring occasionally, until the sugar is dissolved and the liquid turns clear. Use a pastry brush dipped in water to wash any remaining sugar crystals down the side of the pan. Stick a candy thermometer into the pot, increase the heat to medium-high, and cook without stirring until the mixture thickens and your thermometer reads 230°F. Add the pecans and butter, and, stirring constantly, cook until the mixture reaches 305°F. Remove from the heat, and quickly stir in the baking soda and vanilla. Be careful, as the mixture will sputter and foam.

4 Pour the mixture in 3 equal portions onto the buttered baking sheets. Butter the back of a wooden spoon, and use it to spread the mixture as thinly as possible. Evenly sprinkle the sea salt over the brittle. Allow to cool, and then break into pieces. Store in an airtight container for up to a month.

CHILE-SPICED Hot Fudge Sauce MAKES 2 CUPS

MEXICAN CHEFS HAVE known forever how well chiles and chocolate work together, in both savory and sweet foods. Here, just the right spike of chile flavor and heat combine to make a tongue-tingling sauce for a sundae.

1½ cups heavy cream

½ cup sugar

½ vanilla bean, split lengthwise and scraped

1¼ cups unsweetened cocoa powder (not Dutch processed)

Generous ½ teaspoon ancho chile powder

¼ teaspoon chipotle chile powder

Pinch of ground cardamom

¼ teaspoon table salt

Put a large, heavy-bottomed saucepan over medium heat; add the cream, sugar, and vanilla bean and seeds; and heat to dissolve the sugar, stirring occasionally, about 5 minutes. Whisk in the cocoa powder, chile powders, cardamom, and salt. Increase the heat to medium-high, and slowly bring the sauce to a low boil, whisking constantly. Reduce the heat, and simmer gently until shiny, 5 minutes. Remove the vanilla bean. Serve hot or chill and reheat before serving.

WHITE SANGRIA Peach Compote

MAKES A LITTLE MORE THAN 2 CUPS

THE FLAVORS of white sangria dispelled into a dessert, this is beautiful over vanilla ice cream with pound cake or shortbread.

½ cup dry white wine

⅓ cup sugar

2 cups chopped, peeled peaches

1 tablespoon unsalted butter

1 teaspoon grated lemon zest

1 tablespoon fresh lemon juice

1 tablespoon brandy

1 tablespoon Cointreau

In a small saucepan, bring the wine, sugar, and peaches to a boil, reduce the heat, and simmer until the fruit is softened and the mixture is slightly thickened, about 10 minutes. Swirl in the butter, and remove from the heat. Add the lemon zest and juice, brandy, and Cointreau. Refrigerate until serving.

In winter, substitute 1 (10-ounce) bag frozen peach slices for the fresh peaches.

COCONUT-HONEY **Marshmallows**

IF YOU HAVEN'T made homemade marshmallows—or, worse, haven't *tasted* them—this recipe is a must. Fluffy, gooey-creamy pillows of sweetness, but a bit less sweetness than the bagged, factory variety, made deeply special with the yumminess and slight crunchy texture of toasted coconut.

2 cups unsweetened, shredded dried coconut

Canola oil

3 (¼-ounce) envelopes unflavored gelatin

1½ cups sugar

¾ cup honey

½ teaspoon table salt

1 tablespoon pure vanilla extract

1 Position a rack in the middle of the oven and preheat the oven to 350°F.

2 Scatter the coconut on a baking sheet, and toast, stirring occasionally, until fragrant and golden, 5 to 7 minutes.

3 Coat a 9 × 9-inch baking pan with oil. Sprinkle ½ cup of the toasted coconut onto the bottom of the pan.

4 Pour ½ cup water in the bowl of a stand mixer fitted with the whisk attachment. Sprinkle the gelatin over the water.

5 Combine the sugar, honey, salt, and ½ cup water in a medium saucepan over medium heat. Stir occasionally until the sugar is dissolved. Use a pastry brush dipped in water to wash any sugar crystals down the side of the pan. Increase the heat to medium-high and, without stirring, bring the mixture to a boil. Stick a candy thermometer into the pan, and boil until the mixture reaches 250°F. Remove from the heat.

6 Turn the mixer onto low speed, and slowly pour the hot sugar mixture down the inside of the bowl. Increase the speed to high, and mix until very thick and white, 5 to 10 minutes. Add the vanilla, and mix until thoroughly combined. Pour into the prepared pan, and use wet fingers to smooth the top of the marshmallow. Sprinkle ½ cup of the toasted coconut on top, and allow to cool completely.

7 Run a sharp knife around the edge of the pan to loosen the marshmallow. Invert the pan onto a cutting board to remove. Cut marshmallows into 1½-inch strips, and then to cut the strips into 1½-inch squares. Roll the cut edges in the remaining 1 cup toasted coconut so the marshmallows are covered on all sides.

Marshmallows keep for a month at room temperature in an airtight container.

GRAPEFRUIT AND CAMPARI **Sorbet** MAKES ABOUT 1 QUART

WE LIKE TO SERVE this palate cleanser as a primer for the dessert course, or as a refreshing summer treat. The Italian orange liqueur Campari pairs beautifully with tart grapefruit juice.

¼ cup sugar

3 cups freshly squeezed red grapefruit juice

¼ cup Campari bitter orange liqueur

1 Combine the sugar and ¼ cup water in a small saucepan. Heat over medium heat, stirring occasionally, until the sugar is completely dissolved and the liquid is clear. Remove from the heat and allow to cool. Measure out ¼ cup; reserve any extra simple syrup for sweetening lemonade, iced tea, or cocktails.

2 Stir together the grapefruit juice, Campari, and the ¼ cup simple syrup. Follow the directions on your ice cream maker to freeze.

Unlike ice cream, which is best when "ripened" in the freezer for a few hours, sorbets are best served right out of the ice cream maker.

If you don't have an ice cream maker, make granita instead of sorbet. Just pour the mixture into a shallow baking dish, cover with plastic wrap, and freeze. Every half hour, remove from the freezer, and stir with a fork to break up the ice. The goal is for the mixture to freeze into large, loose crystals, not a block of ice. After 3 to 4 hours, you should have crystals that will keep for up to 3 days in an airtight container.

SOUR CHERRY Cobbler SERVES 8

SOUR CHERRIES ARE a precious commodity. The season is a scant two or three weeks in early summer, and once it's over, it can be difficult to find them frozen; to top it all off, jarred sour cherries are often packed with sugar syrup. Here, Barry's recipe celebrates the flavor of fresh sour cherries with little to distract, except for the best cherry complement out there: almonds.

½ cup almonds

6 cups sour cherries, pitted

1 cup plus 1 tablespoon sugar

1 cup plus 2 tablespoons all-purpose flour

½ cup old-fashioned rolled oats

2 teaspoons baking powder

2 large eggs, lightly beaten

6 tablespoons unsalted butter, melted

1 Preheat the oven to 400°F.

2 Spread the almonds on a baking sheet, and toast in the oven until fragrant, 5 to 7 minutes. Let cool, and then chop coarsely.

3 In a medium saucepan, combine the cherries and ¼ cup of the sugar. Heat over medium heat until the sugar has melted and the cherries are heated through, about 10 minutes. Remove from the heat, sprinkle 2 tablespoons of the flour over the mixture, and stir. Pour into a 9 × 9-inch baking dish.

4 In a medium bowl, thoroughly combine the remaining 1 cup flour, ¾ cup of the sugar, the oats, and baking powder. Pour in the beaten eggs, and use your fingers to incorporate until you have lumps of batter. Evenly distribute the batter over the cherries. Sprinkle with the toasted almonds, pour the butter over the mixture, and sprinkle the remaining 1 tablespoon sugar evenly on top.

5 Bake until the juice is bubbling, and the batter is golden brown, 15 to 20 minutes. Allow to cool at least slightly on a wire rack; serve warm or at room temperature.

Pistachio Chews WITH CHOCOLATE GANACHE FILLING   MAKES 1 DOZEN SANDWICH COOKIES

THERE IS NOTHING Barry and I like more in a cookie than chewiness. Having become firmly addicted to a delightfully chewy, fudgy, chocolate-walnut cookie by the famous baker François Payard, Barry embarked on a mission to create a pistachio cookie with similar properties. A dozen or so batches later, here is the result. They're great on their own, but become even more fabulous when made into a sandwich cookie with a chocolate ganache filling. Add a scoop of vanilla, chocolate, or salted caramel ice cream, and wow, is dessert ever served!

1 cup raw, shelled pistachios

2 large egg whites, room temperature

⅛ teaspoon table salt

1 cup sugar

¼ cup all-purpose flour

1 tablespoon pure vanilla extract

¼ cup heavy cream

6 ounces high-quality bittersweet chocolate, melted and warm

1 Position the racks in the oven to divide it into thirds and preheat the oven to 325°F. Line two baking sheets with parchment paper.

2 On another baking sheet, toast the pistachios until fragrant, 5 to 8 minutes, watching them carefully so they don't burn. Let cool, and then chop them in a food processor until coarse.

3 Using a stand mixer with the whisk attachment on medium-high speed, beat the egg whites and salt until they form stiff peaks. Reduce the speed to medium and gradually add the sugar and then the pistachios. Mix in the flour and vanilla. The batter will be soupy.

4 Use a 1¼-inch ice cream scoop to drop batter onto the prepared baking sheets, spacing the cookies 2 inches apart (the batter will spread slightly when dropped on the baking sheet). Bake until slightly golden, 10 to 12 minutes, rotating and reversing the baking sheets halfway through. Allow the cookies to cool slightly on the baking sheet; then slide the parchment onto a rack to cool completely.

5 To make the ganache, gradually whisk the cream into the chocolate, and allow the mixture to cool until spreadable.

6 Peel the cookies from the parchment, and sandwich together with ganache filling.

Rustic Apricot Tart WITH
TOASTED ALMONDS MAKES 1 (13-INCH) TART; SERVES 8 TO 10

THIS BEAUTIFUL TART looks like something that should be served at a country house in Provence. Yet anybody can make it—count those ingredients, please! It also responds to a welcome trend in dessert-making these days: being more thoughtful about added sugar, which is to say using a bit less of it. Of course, no two apricots are alike; taste the fruit filling before you bake, and adjust sweetness as needed.

CRUST

2 cups plus 3 tablespoons all-purpose flour, plus more for rolling

¼ cup plus 1 tablespoon sugar

½ teaspoon table salt

12 tablespoons (1½ sticks) unsalted butter, cut into small pieces, cold

1 large egg

2 large egg yolks

1½ teaspoons fresh lemon juice

1 teaspoon pure vanilla extract

FILLING

½ cup sliced almonds

5 tablespoons sugar

2¼ pounds fresh apricots, halved and pitted

1 Make the crust: Combine the flour, sugar, and salt in a large bowl, and stir together. Cut in the butter until the mixture looks like coarse crumbs. In a small bowl, whisk together the egg, egg yolks, lemon juice, and vanilla. Add to the flour and butter and knead until the mixture comes together and forms a ball. Cover with plastic wrap and refrigerate for at least 1 hour.

2 Meanwhile, prepare the filling: Heat a large skillet over medium-high heat, add the almonds, and toast them until they are just starting to brown, about 2 minutes. (I don't recommend taking your eye off the skillet for even a second at this stage; I've burned my share of almonds.) Reduce the heat to medium, add 2 tablespoons of the sugar, and cook until the sugar melts and glazes the nuts,

(recipe continues)

Don't forget the
dessert wine. This
tart pairs really
nicely with, say, the
Château d'Yquem
Sauternes in the
photo—or, for a
less pricey option,
ice wine from
Inniskillin.

3 to 4 minutes. Remove from the heat and pour the nuts onto a plate to cool.

3 Preheat the oven to 425°F.

4 On a lightly floured surface, roll out the dough into an 18-inch circle. Then transfer to a baking sheet by rolling the dough onto the rolling pin and unrolling it onto the sheet. Take 2 tablespoons of the toasted almonds and, leaving a 2½-inch border, sprinkle them over the dough. Next, place the apricots, cut side down, in circles over the almonds. Sprinkle the rest of the almonds over the apricots. Then, making a pleat every 4 to 5 inches as you go, fold the border of dough over the apricots, leaving a hole in the middle of the tart. Sprinkle the remaining 3 tablespoons sugar over the tart, and transfer to the oven.

5 Bake until the crust is golden brown and the filling is bubbly, 30 to 35 minutes. Let cool for at least 10 minutes before cutting into wedges and serving.

Sweet Avocado Mousse WITH MANGO AND BLUEBERRY SAUCE SERVES 6

YES—AVOCADO FOR DESSERT! The rich and creamy texture of avocado is actually commonly used in desserts in some countries, especially in South America, and especially in mousses. Ripe mango adds another layer of mellow sweetness; lemon juice and zest brighten the flavors. Meanwhile, a simple berry sauce adds more vivid flavor and color to the plate.

BLUEBERRY SAUCE

½ cup sugar

1 teaspoon grated lemon zest

1 pint blueberries

1½ tablespoons fresh lemon juice

AVOCADO MOUSSE

1 large ripe mango

3 ripe Hass avocadoes

¾ cup whole milk

1½ cups sugar

1 tablespoon grated lemon zest

¼ cup fresh lemon juice

¼ teaspoon fine sea salt

1½ cups heavy cream

1 Make the sauce: In a small pan, combine the sugar and lemon zest with ½ cup water over medium heat. Simmer for 5 minutes to dissolve the sugar completely. Add the blueberries, and simmer until they begin to break down, 8 to 10 minutes. Remove from the heat, add the lemon juice, and chill completely in the refrigerator.

2 Make the mousse: Peel, pit, and chop the mango. You need about 1 cup mango. Put it into a food processor. Halve and pit the avocadoes, and spoon the flesh into the food processor. Add the milk, sugar, lemon zest and juice, and salt, and puree until smooth.

3 In a stand mixer with the whisk attachment, whip the cream until it just holds stiff peaks. Fold the avocado mixture into the cream.

4 Pour some sauce onto each of 6 plates and spoon some avocado mousse next to it.

SHOWSTOPPING TRIPLE-LAYER Meyer Lemon Cake

MAKES 1 (9-INCH) LAYER CAKE; SERVES 12

THIS CAKE IS the most elegant and pretty dessert in this book, and one every bit delicious enough to justify the effort it takes. Making the candy garnish and curd filling in addition to the cake and frosting can turn this into a project. But for a special occasion, or if you're just in the mood to show off your pastry prowess, nothing beats this tall, three-layer beauty full of the bright flavor of Meyer lemons. Barry likes to serve a palate cleanser before this cake, joking with guests that he wants to remove the taste of my cooking from their palates. Cute.

CANDIED MEYER LEMON PEEL

5 Meyer lemons, preferably organic

2½ cups sugar

MEYER LEMON CURD

2 teaspoons unflavored powdered gelatin

¾ cup fresh Meyer lemon juice

1½ cups sugar

9 large egg yolks

2 tablespoons grated Meyer lemon zest

¼ teaspoon table salt

12 tablespoons (1½ sticks) unsalted butter, cubed

CAKE

12 tablespoons (1½ sticks) unsalted butter, plus more for the pans, at room temperature

2¾ cups cake flour, plus more for the pans

1⅔ cups sugar

1 tablespoon baking powder

1 teaspoon table salt

4 large egg whites

2 large eggs

1 cup whole milk

1 tablespoon pure vanilla extract

1 teaspoon grated Meyer lemon zest

FROSTING

1 (8-ounce) package cream cheese, at room temperature

8 tablespoons (1 stick) unsalted butter, at room temperature

1¾ cups confectioners' sugar

You will need to buy about 7 lemons for this recipe. If Meyers are unavailable, regular lemons work fine.

(recipe continues)

1 Make the candied Meyer lemon peel: Cut 1/4 inch off the tops and bottoms of the lemons. Score the peels vertically, dividing into 4 even strips. Peel off each quarter. Slice the peels lengthwise into 1/4-inch-thick strips. (Juice the lemons and save the juice for the curd.)

2 In a small saucepan over high heat, bring 4 cups water to a boil. Add the lemon peels, and boil for 2 minutes. Drain in a colander, and rinse peels with cold water. Repeat this blanching process 2 more times.

3 Rinse out the saucepan. Add 3 cups water and 2 cups of the sugar, return to high heat, and stir until the sugar dissolves and the mixture is boiling. Reduce the heat to low, add the lemon peels, and simmer gently for 1 hour, stirring occasionally, until the peels are candied and soft.

4 Remove the pan from the heat, and allow the mixture to cool. Remove the peels with a slotted spoon, and dry on a rack set over a baking pan. Once dry, toss the peels with the remaining 1/2 cup sugar to coat, and store in an airtight container at room temperature for up to 1 week.

5 Make the Meyer lemon curd: Sprinkle the gelatin over 1/4 cup of the Meyer lemon juice, and let sit for 15 minutes.

6 In a medium saucepan, whisk together the sugar, egg yolks, remaining 1/2 cup lemon juice, lemon zest, and salt until combined. Add the butter, and whisk over medium heat until the mixture thickens and starts to bubble around the edges, 8 to 10 minutes, being careful not to allow the mixture to boil.

7 Remove from the heat, and whisk in the gelatin mixture until smooth. Transfer to a small heatproof bowl, press plastic wrap against the surface of the mixture to prevent a skin from forming, and refrigerate the curd until cold.

(recipe continues)

8   Make the cake: Position two racks to divide the oven into thirds, and preheat the oven to 350°F. Butter and flour 3 (9-inch) round cake pans.

9   In an electric stand mixer with the paddle attachment, blend the flour, sugar, baking powder, and salt until well combined. Add the butter, and mix on medium speed for several minutes, until crumbs start to come together. Add the egg whites one at a time, then eggs one at a time, mixing for 2 minutes between each addition, and scraping down the bowl after every other addition. Add the milk one-third at a time, mixing for 2 minutes between each addition, and adding the vanilla and zest with the last third of the milk. Scrape down the bowl with a spatula.

10 Divide the batter evenly between the pans (a kitchen scale is useful for this), and bake until a toothpick inserted in the center of each cake comes out clean, 20 to 25 minutes, carefully turning and rotating the pans halfway through baking. Cool the cakes for 5 minutes on a rack, remove them from the pans, and cool completely on the rack.

11 Make the frosting: In an electric stand mixer with the paddle attachment, beat together the cream cheese, butter, and ¾ cup of the lemon curd. Slowly add the confectioners' sugar, and beat until combined and fluffy.

12 Assemble the cake: On the first cake layer, spread half of the remaining lemon curd. Top with the second cake layer, and spread with the remaining curd. Top with the third cake layer, and frost the top and sides with the frosting. Decorate the top with candied lemon peel.

GINGER-PUMPKIN Doughnut Holes WITH CARAMEL SAUCE

MAKES 24 HOLES; SERVES 6

ZEPPOLE, FRY BREAD, beignets, elephant ears—every cuisine has its version of fried dough. Of course, deep-frying is not something most of us want to do every day, nor probably should we, but the fact is, there are flavors and textures that can't be accomplished with any other technique, and those flavors and textures are goooood. For this slightly more elegant take on a humble delicacy, Barry arranges a few doughnut holes like a stack of cannon balls, adds a scoop of vanilla ice cream to the side, and tops everything with a drizzle of golden caramel. A sprinkle of toasted nuts and freshly grated nutmeg and cinnamon doesn't hurt, either!

¾ cup plus 1 tablespoon all-purpose flour, plus more for rolling

1 teaspoon baking powder

¼ teaspoon table salt

¼ teaspoon ground cinnamon

¼ teaspoon ground nutmeg

¼ cup packed light brown sugar

1 tablespoon unsalted butter, at room temperature

⅓ cup canned or mashed cooked pumpkin

2 tablespoons buttermilk

1 large egg yolk

1 tablespoon grated fresh peeled ginger

½ teaspoon pure vanilla extract

Canola oil, for frying

Vanilla ice cream, homemade (page 221) or store-bought, for serving, optional

Caramel Sauce (recipe follows)

The dessert works fine with canned pumpkin, but nothing beats fresh. Just split a small pie pumpkin, poke the skin with a fork in several places, place cut side up on a baking sheet, and roast at 350°F for 1½ to 2 hours, depending on the size, until a fork easily goes through the skin and flesh. Cool, scoop the flesh into a sieve, and drain excess water. Puree in a food processor until smooth.

(recipe continues)

It's important to keep the frying oil near 365°F. Higher temperatures will cook the outside of the doughnut holes before the inside is done. Lower temperatures will produce oil-soaked doughnut holes. A small deep fryer with a thermostat eliminates the guesswork of maintaining the optimal temperature, but carefully monitoring a frying thermometer in 2 inches of oil in a cast-iron skillet or Dutch oven on the stovetop works well, too.

1 In a medium bowl, whisk together the flour, baking powder, salt, cinnamon, and nutmeg until thoroughly combined.

2 In the bowl of a stand mixer using the paddle attachment on medium-high speed, beat together the brown sugar and butter. Add the pumpkin, buttermilk, egg yolk, ginger, and vanilla, and beat until well combined.

3 Using a spatula, fold in the flour mixture one-third at a time. The result should be a sticky ball of dough. Cover with plastic wrap and refrigerate until cold, 1 to 2 hours, which will make the dough easier to handle.

4 Dust a counter with flour, and use a floured rolling pin to roll the dough into a ½-inch-thick disk. A 1½-inch circular cutter is ideal for doughnut holes. Dip the cutter in flour to prevent dough from sticking, cut out holes, and transfer them to a baking sheet lined with parchment paper. Form the scraps into another ball, roll, and repeat.

5 Heat the canola oil to 365°F. (If you don't have a frying thermometer, use the popcorn method to tell when the oil is at a good temperature for frying: Drop a kernel of popping corn in the oil as it heats. It will pop when the oil is between 350°F and 365°F.) Working in batches, use a slotted spoon or fry basket to carefully lower 6 holes into the oil, and fry, turning halfway, until deep golden brown, about 5 minutes. Using a slotted spoon, remove the holes from the oil, and drain on paper towels, turning them so the towels absorb as much excess oil as possible.

6 Stack a few doughnut holes per plate, and add a scoop of ice cream to the side, if desired. Drizzle with caramel sauce, and serve immediately.

Caramel Sauce MAKES 1½ CUPS

1 cup sugar

½ cup heavy cream

1 teaspoon pure vanilla extract

1 Put the sugar and ½ cup water in a heavy saucepan over low heat. Cook, stirring, until the sugar dissolves (the liquid will turn clear), 1 to 2 minutes. Turn the heat up to medium and cook, swirling the pan occasionally for even cooking, until the sugar syrup turns a caramel color, about 20 minutes.

2 When the syrup turns a dark amber color, remove the pan from the heat, and carefully pour in the cream. Stand back, as the caramel will sputter. Continue to stir, and return to low heat if necessary to melt the caramel. Once the sauce is smooth, remove from the heat, and stir in the vanilla.

Breakfast and Brunch

CAMPARI AÇAÍ Brunch Punch SERVES 6

HERE, A GROWN-UP punch that packs the wonderful, slightly bitter flavor of Campari, one of my favorite tastes. Using frozen juices to chill the punch prevents it from getting watery—and freezing herbs inside those juices is attractive and chic.

2 cups tangerine or orange juice, no pulp, cold

2 cups 100% juice cranberry juice, cold

6 sprigs of basil or mint

½ cup açaí juice, cold

1 cup white rum or vodka, cold

½ cup Campari bitter orange liqueur, cold

Slices of lime, orange, and lemon, for garnish

1 The night before, pour 1 cup of the tangerine and 1 cup of the cranberry juice into 2 small, uncovered food storage containers. Place the basil sprigs in the juices, and transfer to the freezer.

2 Pop the frozen tangerine and cranberry juices out of their containers and into a half-gallon pitcher. Add the remaining 1 cup tangerine juice, remaining 1 cup cranberry juice, the açaí juice, white rum, and Campari, and garnish with slices of lime, orange, and lemon.

Açaí juice, from the Brazilian rainforest's açaí berry, adds a bit of intrigue (as well as antioxidants); it's now widely available. If you can't find it, add more cranberry or tangerine juice.

FIRE ISLAND **Sunset** SERVES 1

SWEET-TART GRAPEFRUIT, exotic hibiscus, bracing tequila—a great kick-start for Sunday.

Ice

½ cup fresh pink grapefruit juice, cold

¼ cup brewed hibiscus tea, cold

¼ cup silver tequila

½ teaspoon Cointreau

1 thin slice or chunk candied ginger

Fill a tall glass with ice, add the grapefruit juice, tea, tequila, and Cointreau, and stir. Garnish with the ginger.

THE **Wildflower** SERVES 1

I WHIPPED THIS UP for my friends at the Robert Mondavi Winery, for whom I've done media and education work for five years. Robert Mondavi wines are really too good to mix with anything—yet, the better your ingredients are going in, the better the final result, so why not? This is a great, crisp summer refresher. The St. Germain elderflower liqueur is gloriously floral.

1 sprig of lavender or mint

Ice

½ cup light, dry white wine, cold

¼ cup St. Germain elderflower liqueur, cold

¼ cup vodka, cold

Club soda, cold

Pick a few of the lavender buds from the bottom of the sprig, and muddle them in a highball glass. Fill the glass with ice, pour in the wine, liqueur, and vodka, and top with club soda. Garnish with the lavender sprig.

Banana-Fig Bread MAKES 1 (9-INCH) LOAF

WE BUY BANANAS, we eat a few, and the rest turn black. So we toss them in the freezer for use in smoothies and quick breads. Here's one of the latter, which Barry made new and earthy with the addition of figs, and enriched with tangy yogurt.

6 tablespoons (¾ cup) unsalted butter, melted and cooled, plus more for the pan

1⅓ cups all-purpose flour, plus more for the pan

1 cup walnuts

⅔ cup whole-wheat flour, preferably whole-wheat pastry flour

½ cup granulated sugar

½ cup packed light brown sugar

1 teaspoon baking soda

½ teaspoon table salt

3 large or 4 medium very ripe bananas

1½ cups dried figs, stemmed and cut into ¼-inch pieces

⅓ cup plain yogurt

2 large eggs

2 teaspoons pure vanilla extract

1 Preheat the oven to 350°F. Butter and flour a 9 × 5-inch loaf pan.

2 Toast the walnuts on a baking sheet in the oven until golden and fragrant, 5 to 10 minutes, watching carefully so they don't burn. Set aside to cool.

3 Whisk together the flours, sugars, baking soda, and salt in a medium bowl until thoroughly combined. In another bowl, mash the bananas, figs, yogurt, eggs, butter, and vanilla until combined and chunky. Stir in the walnuts.

4 Fold the banana mixture into the dry ingredients until just combined. Pour the batter into the loaf pan. Bake until a toothpick inserted in the middle comes out clean, about 55 minutes. Cool in the pan on a rack for 30 minutes; then unmold and cool completely.

Brunch Tart WITH SWISS CHARD, BACON, AND LEEK SERVES 8 AS AN APPETIZER OR BRUNCH ITEM

A LUXURIOUS, savory tart that's easy to put together and that puffs up gorgeously in the oven, this works beautifully for brunch or lunch; pair it with a simple green salad dressed with a light vinaigrette. This is a rare example of a recipe in which I use a premade ingredient—that's only because I don't tend to have three days to make my own puff pastry. I like the Dufour brand; it has only natural, high-quality ingredients, and no preservatives. It's great to have around, both for desserts and savory treats like this tart, or, say, pot pies.

6 slices of bacon, cut crosswise into ¼-inch strips

2 fat leeks (white and pale parts only), coarsely chopped and washed

½ medium yellow onion, chopped

2 garlic cloves, chopped

1 pound Swiss chard, ribs removed, coarsely chopped

Kosher salt and freshly ground black pepper

1 (15-ounce) container ricotta

3 large eggs

1 teaspoon thyme leaves

All-purpose flour, for rolling

1 sheet frozen puff pastry, thawed in the refrigerator

1 In a large sauté pan, fry the bacon over medium-low heat until brown and crispy. Drain on paper towels and set aside. Reserve the fat in the pan.

2 Add the leeks and onion to the pan and cook over medium heat, stirring occasionally, until wilted, 5 minutes. Add the garlic, stir, and cook until fragrant, 1 minute. Add the chard and cook until wilted and tender, 5 minutes. Remove from the heat, taste, and season with salt and pepper as needed; let cool.

3 Meanwhile, in a large bowl, whisk together the ricotta, 2 of the eggs, the thyme, and ½ teaspoon salt. Then, fold the cooled vegetable mixture and the bacon into the ricotta mixture.

Swap the bacon for ½ cup freshly grated Parmesan or pitted kalamata olives, and you have a vegetarian dish.

Replace the chard with spinach, kale, or (with a longer sauté time of 20 minutes and a finer cut) collards.

(recipe continues)

4 Preheat the oven to 375°F.

5 On a lightly floured surface, roll out the pastry until it's 12 inches square. Using a 12-inch plate or just eyeballing it, cut the dough into a circle (knead scraps into a ball and save for another use—Cheddar straws, say). Transfer the dough to a parchment-lined baking sheet. Spoon the tart filling into the center, leaving a 2-inch border of pastry. Lift the pastry edge and fold over onto the filling, creasing the dough as needed, and leaving a 5-inch circle (or so) of filling exposed. In a small bowl, whisk the remaining egg with 1 tablespoon water, and brush a thin layer of egg wash on the exposed pastry, taking care not to let egg run down the sides to the pan.

6 Bake until the pastry is golden brown, about 45 minutes. Remove from the oven, and let rest for 10 minutes before serving.

Potato Bagels WITH
BUTTER-GLAZED ONIONS   MAKES 12 BAGELS

IF YOU ARE NOT in New York City, it is difficult—some might say impossible—to find a good bagel. If you *are* in New York, there are plenty of people rarin' to argue about where this mythical bread product is best obtained (me, I'm partial to the just-baked egg bagels at Ess-A-Bagel on 1st Avenue at 22nd Street). Wherever you are, it's really interesting to make bagels yourself, even if only once, to understand what makes them so dense, shiny, and good. Here, I take things a step further by introducing the moisture and sweetness (and potassium, vitamin C, and golden color) of Yukon gold potatoes. And just a touch of onion. Give it a schmear of whipped cream cheese, if you like. I like.

1 medium Yukon gold potato (about 5 ounces), scrubbed

4½ cups all-purpose flour, plus more for kneading

1 package active dry yeast

3 teaspoons kosher salt

¼ cup extra-virgin olive oil, plus more for the bowl

2 tablespoons honey

1½ cups diced sweet onion

1 tablespoon unsalted butter

1 large egg beaten with 1 tablespoon water

1 In a large pot, bring 2½ quarts water to a boil, add the potato, whole, and cook until tender, 20 to 25 minutes. Drain, reserving the cooking water. When the potato is cool enough to handle, peel, and then mash to a smooth consistency, adding a few drops of the cooking water if needed.

2 Into the bowl of a stand mixer with the dough hook attached, sift the flour, yeast, and 2½ teaspoons of the salt.

3 In a small bowl, mix together the mashed potato, olive oil, and honey. With the mixer motor running on low, add the mashed potato mixture to the flour mixture; then add ½ cup of the potato cooking water. Increase the speed to medium and mix for 10 minutes. If the mixture seems dry, add 1 more teaspoon potato water, and continue to mix for another couple of minutes. Put the dough on a lightly floured surface, and knead by hand until smooth and the dough bounces back when poked, about 5 minutes.

4 Drizzle a little olive oil into a large bowl to coat the bottom. Add the dough, and turn it to coat with oil. Cover the bowl with a damp dish cloth, and leave the dough to rest in a warm spot until doubled in size, 1½ to 2 hours.

(recipe continues)

5 While the dough rises, cook the onion in the butter in a large skillet over low heat until transparent and soft but not browned, 20 to 30 minutes. Season with the remaining 1/2 teaspoon salt, and set aside.

6 Preheat the oven to 450°F.

7 Once the dough has risen, punch it down and form into 12 equal-sized balls. Roll each ball into a rope 6 to 8 inches long, form this into a circle, making sure to pinch the edges closed; wetting them slightly will help to keep them together. Place on a parchment-lined baking sheet, cover with a damp dish cloth, and let rise for 30 minutes.

8 Meanwhile, bring the remaining potato cooking water back to a full boil. After the bagels have rested, place them a few at a time in the boiling water, and cook for 30 seconds on each side. Remove with a slotted spoon to a rack to drain; then return to the baking sheet.

9 Once all the bagels have been boiled, transfer the baking sheet to the oven and bake for 10 minutes. Brush each bagel with egg wash and top with 1/2 teaspoon of the sautéed onion. Return to the oven and bake until golden brown, 10 to 15 minutes. Let cool for at least 15 minutes before serving.

Poached Emmenthaler Eggs WITH GRILLED BREAD SERVES 2 TO 4

WHAT'S BETTER THAN sopping up warm, runny egg yolk with crispy, grilled bread? Sopping up warm, runny egg with melted cheese on it with crispy, grilled bread. This little snack was inspired by a dish of brilliant chef and *Chopped* judge Scott Conant's (or stolen, you might say; of course, Scott, being Scott, uses fancy duck eggs and some sort of pricier cheese). You can also dress up the eggs some more with a little roasted garlic or fresh herbs.

4 (1-inch-thick) slices whole-grain crusty bread

Olive oil

Kosher salt and freshly ground pepper

4 jumbo eggs

½ cup grated Emmenthaler cheese

1 Preheat the oven to 350°F.

2 Brush each slice of bread with olive oil on both sides. In a skillet, under a broiler, or on an indoor grill heated to medium-high, toast each side until golden brown. Set aside.

3 Fill a 12-inch saucepan with about an inch of water, and heat to boiling. Reduce the heat so that the water simmers, and add ½ teaspoon salt.

4 Crack each egg into its own separate, small bowl and season with salt and pepper. Slip the eggs gently into the simmering water. Cook until the whites are set and the yolks are still very runny, 2 minutes.

5 Remove the eggs with a slotted spoon and place in individual ovenproof ramekins. Sprinkle with the cheese and bake until the cheese melts, about 5 minutes. Serve immediately, with the bread.

ROMESCO, MANCHEGO, AND IBÉRICO **Omelet** SERVES 2

SOME PEOPLE SAY Spanish cuisine is the next Italian in this country; whether or not that's true, the Catalan classic Romesco is a sauce you need to know. Versatile, easy to make, and unique, it's based largely on ground nuts and roasted red peppers, thickened with bread and made pungent with garlic and vinegar. Tomatoes are common. Some cooks use fennel or mint, too, particularly where seafood is concerned. Here, it brings life and color to an omelet with the great Spanish ham, *jamón ibérico,* and nutty, crumbly Manchego cheese. Also try the sauce with chicken or fish, or thinned out to make a vinaigrette.

¼ cup pine nuts

⅓ cup extra-virgin olive oil, plus more if needed

¼ cup roasted almonds

1 (½-inch-thick) slice bread, cut into ½-inch cubes

2 garlic cloves, sliced

Pinch of red pepper flakes, or more to taste

1 canned, peeled whole tomato

¼ cup drained jarred roasted red peppers, preferably piquillos or pimientos

1 tablespoon red wine vinegar

Kosher salt

5 large eggs

1 scallion (white and green parts), finely chopped

½ cup coarsely grated Manchego cheese

3 slices *jamón ibérico* or Serrano ham

1 Preheat the oven to 350°F.

2 Toast the pine nuts on a baking sheet in the oven until golden, 10 to 15 minutes.

3 In a 9-inch, nonstick sauté pan, warm the olive oil over medium heat. Add the pine nuts, almonds, bread, garlic, and red pepper flakes, and cook until the garlic and bread are golden brown, about 3 minutes. Transfer to a food processor with the tomato, roasted red peppers, vinegar, and ¼ teaspoon salt, and pulse until smooth. Add 1 to 3 tablespoons water and a little more oil if the sauce is too thick to pour. Taste for seasoning, and add more salt and red pepper flakes, if needed.

4 In a bowl, whisk the eggs with a pinch of salt, and then blend in the scallion. Reheat the sauté pan over medium heat. Add a little more oil, if needed. Slowly pour the eggs into the pan and cook, using a spatula to loosen the edges and allow uncooked egg to run under, about 3 minutes. Sprinkle the Manchego evenly over the omelet, then put an even layer of ham on just one side, and cover the ham with about ¼ cup Romesco sauce. Cook until the cheese is melted and the omelet is set, 2 to 3 minutes more. Fold the omelet over onto itself with a spatula, cut in half, and transfer to plates. Serve with a dollop of Romesco on top.

Summer Pasta Salad WITH
RIPE TOMATOES AND PEACHES SERVES 4

THIS IS A GREAT brunch dish, colorful and fresh. Use any pasta you want, but I like large elbow macaroni best. For maximum impact, keep the pasta, cheese, tomatoes and peaches, and vinaigrette separate and at room temperature until ready to serve; do not refrigerate, which would dull the lush flavors.

Kosher salt

1 pound dried pasta

5 medium tomatoes, preferably heirloom ones in different colors, at their absolute ripest

3 medium peaches or nectarines, white or yellow, at their absolute ripest

2 tablespoons red wine vinegar

2 garlic cloves, chopped

1 teaspoon red pepper flakes

½ cup extra-virgin olive oil

1 cup ½-inch cubed smoked fresh mozzarella

1 hothouse cucumber, peeled, halved lengthwise, seeded, and sliced ¾ inch thick

¼ cup thinly sliced basil leaves

1 Cook the pasta in generously salted boiling water until just al dente. Drain, and set aside to cool completely.

2 Cut the tomatoes into bite-size chunks, and put them and any juices from the cutting board into a very large bowl. Sprinkle with 1 teaspoon salt, and toss very gently so as not to break up the tomatoes. Allow the salt to draw out the juices for 15 minutes.

3 Peel and stone the peaches, cut into bite-size chunks, and add to the tomatoes. Toss gently to cover the peaches with tomato juice (which will prevent the fruit from browning).

4 Make the vinaigrette: In a small bowl, whisk together the vinegar, garlic, red pepper flakes, and olive oil.

5 When you are ready to serve, add the pasta to the tomato mixture, pour the vinaigrette over, and add the mozzarella, cucumber, and basil. Gently toss to combine. Serve at room temperature.

STICKY BUN **Bread Pudding** SERVES 6

JUST BECAUSE IT'S breakfast (or brunch) doesn't mean you don't need dessert! Here is Barry's simple take on a bread pudding that tastes like the best cinnamon buns you've ever had. Challah bread makes for a great, buttery foundation; if you can't find it, make your own (page 266), or try to use some other soft, eggy, golden bread.

4 large eggs

2 cups plus 2 tablespoons half-and-half, or more if needed

1 teaspoon pure vanilla extract

1 cup chopped pecans

½ cup packed light brown sugar

2½ teaspoons ground cinnamon

8 (1-inch-thick) slices day-old challah, crusts removed

8 tablespoons (1 stick) unsalted butter, at room temperature

1 cup confectioners' sugar

1 Preheat the oven to 350°F.

2 In a medium bowl, whisk the eggs, 2 cups of the half-and-half, and the vanilla to blend.

3 In a small bowl, stir together the pecans, brown sugar, and cinnamon.

4 Butter the bread slices on both sides generously. Place 2 slices of the bread in the bottom of a 9 × 5-inch loaf pan or small baking dish, cutting additional bread pieces to line the bottom of the pan snugly. Sprinkle with one-third of the pecan mixture. Repeat twice, using the remaining bread and pecan mixture. Press on the bread to compact. Pour the egg mixture over the bread by ½ cupfuls, saturating the bread.

5 Put the loaf pan in the center of a 9 × 13-inch baking pan, and transfer to the oven. Carefully pour enough hot water into the baking pan to come halfway up the sides of the loaf pan. Bake until the pudding is set, about 45 minutes. Remove the loaf pan from the water; cool slightly. Turn out the loaf onto a platter.

6 Whisk the confectioners' sugar and the remaining 2 tablespoons half-and-half in a medium bowl to blend, adding more half-and-half if necessary to make a thin glaze. Slice the warm bread pudding thickly, and transfer to plates. Drizzle the bread pudding slices with glaze, and serve.

Little Challah Breads WITH MIXED SEEDS AND SALT MAKES 2 (8-INCH) LOAVES

NOT TO SOUND too much like somebody's dad, but you can learn valuable lessons from bread. In the main, the power of patience: plan ahead, give yourself enough time, and suddenly, there's nothing hard at all about baking the staff o' life—even this twist on the Jewish braided classic. Giving dough enough time to rise and rest makes it supple and easy to work with; giving it an entire day (or up to four) in the fridge slows the fermentation, which allows more flavor to develop. It's a lot like planting a garden or a tree; think of it as an investment, in this case, for tomorrow's dinner. And enjoy the cooks-only pleasure: checking in on your dough once in a while, just to drink in those aromas. After you bake, eat hot with lots of butter and Plummy Quick Jam (opposite).

¾ cup plus 2 tablespoons warm water

2¼ teaspoons active dry yeast

2¼ teaspoons table salt

2 large eggs, lightly beaten

¼ cup honey

4 tablespoons (½ stick) unsalted butter, melted

3½ cups all-purpose flour

1 large egg yolk mixed with 1 teaspoon water

½ teaspoon poppy seeds

½ teaspoon sesame seeds

½ teaspoon kosher or coarse sea salt

1 In a large mixing bowl, stir together the water, yeast, table salt, eggs, honey, and butter. Slowly mix in the flour until it's evenly moistened. The dough will be sticky. Cover with plastic wrap and place in the refrigerator for 1 to 4 days.

2 Divide the dough in half; then, divide each half into three 8-inch ropes. Pinch the top of three of the ropes together and fold the pinch under to hold tightly. Braid the challah, tucking the final end under, too, and place on a baking sheet. Repeat with the remaining dough, placing it several inches from the first loaf on the baking sheet. Cover with a clean tea towel, and allow the loaves to rise for 1½ hours.

3 Preheat the oven to 375°F.

4 Brush the challahs with the egg yolk wash, sprinkle with the poppy and sesame seeds, add the kosher salt, and gently brush again with wash to make sure the seeds stick. Bake until golden brown, 30 to 40 minutes. Cool on a wire rack at least slightly, and serve warm or at room temperature.

PLUMMY **Quick Jam** MAKES 1½ CUPS

THREE INGREDIENTS, LESS than an hour, and you've got the best topping for toast you could imagine—especially in summer, when local plums are at their peak in most parts of the country. This makes a loose, syrupy jam that's also great for glazing meats like duck.

1½ pounds plums, pitted
  and cut into ¼-inch slices

½ cup sugar

½ bay leaf

In a medium saucepan, combine the plums, sugar, and bay leaf. Cook gently over medium heat, stirring occasionally, until thickened and syrupy, 35 to 40 minutes. Remove the bay leaf, cool, and serve, or refrigerate for up to a few weeks.

Acknowledgments

HEARTFELT THANKS to everyone at Clarkson Potter: Doris Cooper, Ashley Phillips, Jane Treuhaft, Stephanie Huntwork, Mark McCauslin, Joan Denman, and my brilliant editor, Rica Allannic; Melissa Vaughn; my literary agent, Jay Mandel, at William Morris Endeavor; and our crackerjack photography team, Barbara Fritz, Jeff Kavanaugh, Jamie Kimm, Gary Noel, Rachel Sutherland, and their fearless leader, Ben Fink, who shot all these beautiful photos in our house with nothing but natural light. To Nathalie Smith at Global Table; The Conran Shop; Ochre furniture; and ABC Carpet and Home.

To our friends and fellow adventurers Chuck Gonzales and Michael Thibeault, Peter Ross, Doug and Jessica Warren, Edward MacDonald and Andrew Landers, Bill Palmer and Patricia Mears, Amy Azzarito, David Riordan, and, especially, Megan Schlow. To our incomparable assistant, Tanner Welsh.

To my friend and *Chopped* creator Linda Lea, everybody at Notional, and our amazing crew. And to our team at Food Network, Bob Tuschman and Kim Williamson, and Maile Carpenter, the brains behind *Food Network Magazine*.

To the Bistro Baron, the Italian Superscribe, the Greenmarket Guru, the Star Executive Chef, the Toast of the Lower East Side, the master of Dynamic American Cooking, the Latin Cuisine Aficionado, and the Rock-n-Roll Chef—better known as our *Chopped* judges, whose wisdom and friendship have made me a better cook: Alex Guarnaschelli, Aarón Sanchez, Amanda Freitag, Geoffrey Zakarian, Chris Santos, Marc Murphy, Maneet Chouhan, Scott Conant, Marcus Samuelsson, Jody Williams, Sue Torres, Zak Palaccio, and Seamus Mullen. I could stand around talking food with great chefs all day—and whaddya know, I do. These acknowledgments brought to you by Summer's . . . well, you know.

To the focal points of our food life in Brooklyn: Fairway, the best grocery anywhere; Harry, Taylor, Ben, Brent, and Tom at The Brooklyn Kitchen/The Meat Hook; Greene Grape Provisions, Choice Market, and Choice Greene; to the helpful folk at Brooklyn Public House; and to Frankie and Vito at Graziela's.

And, of course, ever and always, to my pastry chef, Barry.

Index